M000036041

The

Minimalist

Teacher

The Minimalist Teacher

Tamera Musiowsky-Borneman

C. Y. Arnold

Alexandria, Virginia USA

1703 N. Beauregard St. • Alexandria, VA 22311-1714 USA
Phone: 800-933-2723 or 703-578-9600 • Fax: 703-575-5400
Website: www.ascd.org • E-mail: member@ascd.org
Author guidelines: www.ascd.org/write

Ranjit Sidhu, *CEO & Executive Director;* Penny Reinart, *Chief Impact Officer;* Genny Ostertag, *Senior Director, Acquisitions and Editing;* Allison Scott, *Senior Acquisitions Editor;* Julie Houtz, *Director, Book Editing;* Megan Doyle, *Editor;* Thomas Lytle, *Creative Director;* Donald Ely, *Art Director;* Masie Chong, *Graphic Designer;* Keith Demmons, *Senior Production Designer;* Kelly Marshall, *Production Manager;* Shajuan Martin, *E-Publishing Specialist*

Copyright © 2021 ASCD. All rights reserved. It is illegal to reproduce copies of this work in print or electronic format (including reproductions displayed on a secure intranet or stored in a retrieval system or other electronic storage device from which copies can be made or displayed) without the prior written permission of the publisher. By purchasing only authorized electronic or print editions and not participating in or encouraging piracy of copyrighted materials, you support the rights of authors and publishers. Readers who wish to reproduce or republish excerpts of this work in print or electronic format may do so for a small fee by contacting the Copyright Clearance Center (CCC), 222 Rosewood Dr., Danvers, MA 01923, USA (phone: 978-750-8400; fax: 978-646-8600; web: www.copyright.com). To inquire about site licensing options or any other reuse, contact ASCD Permissions at www.ascd.org/permissions or permissions@ascd.org. For a list of vendors authorized to license ASCD e-books to institutions, see www.ascd.org/epubs. Send translation inquiries to translations@ascd.org.

ASCD® is a registered trademark of the Association for Supervision and Curriculum Development. All other trademarks contained in this book are the property of, and reserved by, their respective owners, and are used for editorial and informational purposes only. No such use should be construed to imply sponsorship or endorsement of the book by the respective owners.

All web links in this book are correct as of the publication date below but may have become inactive or otherwise modified since that time. If you notice a deactivated or changed link, please e-mail books@ascd.org with the words "Link Update" in the subject line. In your message, please specify the web link, the book title, and the page number on which the link appears.

PAPERBACK ISBN: 978-1-4166-3011-1   ASCD product #121058   n7/21
PDF E-BOOK ISBN: 978-1-4166-3012-8; see Books in Print for other formats.
Quantity discounts are available: e-mail programteam@ascd.org or call 800-933-2723, ext. 5773, or 703-575-5773. For desk copies, go to www.ascd.org/deskcopy.

Library of Congress Cataloging-in-Publication Data
Names: Musiowsky-Borneman, Tamera, author. | Arnold, C. Y., author.
Title: The minimalist teacher / Tamera Musiowsky-Borneman and C. Y. Arnold.
Description: Alexandria, Virginia USA : ASCD, [2021] | Includes
    bibliographical references and index.
Identifiers: LCCN 2021014044 (print) | LCCN 2021014045 (ebook) | ISBN
    9781416630111 (paperback) | ISBN 9781416630128 (pdf)
Subjects: LCSH: Classroom management. | Orderliness. | Classroom
    environment. | Teaching.
Classification: LCC LB3013 .M78 2021 (print) | LCC LB3013 (ebook) | DDC
    371.102/4--dc23
LC record available at https://lccn.loc.gov/2021014044
LC ebook record available at https://lccn.loc.gov/2021014045

30 29 28 27 26 25 24 23 22 21   1 2 3 4 5 6 7 8 9 10 11 12

The Minimalist Teacher

Introduction

The Making of Minimalist Teachers in a "Maximum-ist" Society

When conjuring up the image of a minimalist teacher, a few images may come to mind. First, you may think it's not possible. Conversely, you may imagine an expertly organized teacher in an expertly organized space that is highly structured and color-coded with all items in designated places. Or perhaps you imagine a space that is bland and bare, with only the necessities like pencils, paper, and furniture. The reality of creating and living the minimalist approach to teaching and learning in everyday classrooms can stem from these very different ideas, personalities, and personal intricacies, but all with a common purpose.

This book is a result of us coming together after many professional conversations around a common belief about quality teaching and learning. Although our systems of organization are different, and we have some different views for how spaces or resources can be used, our priority is the same—meeting our students' needs effectively and efficiently. A minimal-ist approach to teaching and learning may sound impossible with all the impending demands, or it could be regarded as an overly simplistic way to view quality education. However, simplifying teaching and learning to keep students in our direct line of vision is not oversimplification. It is creating a simplicity that allows education to become richer and more meaningful by way of paring down distractions and all the waste we are faced with daily.

A Culture of Waste

How Did We Get to This Place of Too Much?

Teachers do not need more "stuff" to clutter their space. Where is it written that *more* ever meant *better?* Simply put, it means more work without any guarantee that the learning will be more meaningful or better experienced. What teachers *do* need is support sorting out all the stuff that has been col-lecting inches of dust, shoved into cupboards, and left on shelves over the years. Our personal lives are filled by this systemic culture of waste, which endlessly bleeds into our school lives. We suffer from economic, social, intel-lectual, and time waste that can validate that what we have is just too much.

Paradox of Choice

Restaurants give us such a wide range of options on the menu, but how do you narrow it down without having a slight bout of inner panic? The priority is to eat, and quick, because you are just that hungry. How do you choose which jelly bean to eat first? With a ruffled brow, we put too much thought into something so trivial. Likely no assumptions are made in stating that every educator has been a deer in the headlights, paralyzed with the amount of choice in initiatives, programs, strategies, or tools. In *Paradox of Choice*, Barry Schwartz (2005) speaks about the paralyzing fear of making a choice and understanding the process behind this. He states that "[o]pportunity costs subtract from the satisfaction that we get out of what we choose, even when what we choose is terrific." The additional intellectual waste we face once a choice is made—wondering if the right choice has been made and thinking that another would have been better—causes unneeded stress. This then becomes a good time to think about how choices can be made with effi-ciency and purpose. Once a choice is made, thinking can be decluttered and the initiative can be modified for your particular context.

Too Many Choices

Another effective example of this choice-initiated paralyzing fear has been presented by Malcolm Gladwell. In his TEDTalk "Choice, Happiness and Spaghetti Sauce," Gladwell (2004) speaks about the number of spaghetti sauce choices produced by one spaghetti sauce manufacturer. Offering a few dozen choices does not necessarily mean that people will be drawn to purchase a new sauce. There is comfort in purchasing the one you always buy. You know what it tastes like, how it cooks, and that your family likes it. And what if we try a new flavor and it isn't received well? Your prowess in the kitchen could be called into question, let alone the food, money, and time wasted on this trial of the unknown. We can draw definite parallels between these spaghetti sauce choices to the overabundance of choices in our field. There are so many choices and options in education, it is easy to feel over-whelmed. It is no wonder that educators are drawn back to the ideals and practices they feel are familiar on well-trodden ground.

Likely you have been to an education conference. What do you see at the exhibit hall? Rows upon rows of vendors. Are you drawn to the exhibitors you know? Of course! There is comfort in the known and in returning to practices we have been successful with in the past. However, we need to be cautious of being overly comfortable and less open to innovation. The key when onboarding anything new is to think deeply about what the purpose is, wisely consider your priorities, and be thoughtful about ways to pare down without stripping away the effectiveness of what you are attempting to do.

Cue the Minimalist Movement

People from Japan to the United States and everywhere in between have become fascinated by minimalists, such as Joshua Fields Millburn, Ryan Nicodemus, and Marie Kondo, and their approaches to decluttering spaces. They spark the desire to find purpose and meaning in what takes up space in their physical environments and purge the rest. People are prioritizing life experience over material objects and moving into tiny houses while still recognizing that we cannot do away with all material objects. There is a deli-cate balance in knowing what you need and how you can maximize what you already have to develop a strong sense of commitment to creating a better life.

Additionally, more and more Americans are reading about and prac-ticing meditation to declutter their minds of intellectual waste. Since 2012, there has been a surge in the number of Americans practicing yoga and meditation according to Amy Norton (2018) in her *Health Day News* blog. Increasing numbers of Americans are also getting outdoors to hike, walk, and interact with wildlife according to some U.S. Fish and Wildlife studies (Smith, 2017). And to eliminate mental fatigue, people perform "spring cleaning" of disconnected friends on Facebook to declutter personal relationships. The good news is, we can do the same in our schools and classrooms.

Do Less, Better

Those of us in education might think the idea of doing less seems like an impossible task, as though it is not even a choice. Expectations and duties corner us from every angle of our peripheries and from a wide range of stakeholders. Your students want to schedule a time for class soccer matchups. Your principal is asking to complete the documentation of your assessment results before the break. Parents would like further information about how their children are performing before the next round of standardized assessments. Bulletin board displays of student work are dated from three months prior and have that faded and torn look about them. Your colleague next door is asking you to share what provocation task you are going to use next week to start the new unit of work. How do you say no to these tasks? How do you decide which stakeholder receives your time and effort before the others? How do you find the time to do all of these to-do's justice?

In his book *Essentialism: The Disciplined Pursuit of Less,* Geoff McKeown (2014) proposes that we "do less, better." The proposition is that we find our way to our priorities by paring down to take on more focused tasks and do it better. He describes a filtering process in which we consider our purpose first and foremost, and only say yes to activities that will meet that purpose. He reminds us that remaining in a situation in which we feel like all tasks are vital, that we cannot say no, or that we feel overwhelmed and exhausted actually leads us to be less efficient and poorer performers at our work. So, in fact, our ability to serve our stakeholders decreases as a result of our struggle to meet the needs of all stakeholders efficiently. Joseph Neil (2014), in his book *Less > More,* goes as far as to compare this overwhelmed and frantic state with facing constant failure. When framed in this light, this seems like a defeating and uncomfortable state to exist in. Further to this, in his *New York Times* article "The Unbearable Heaviness of Clutter," Emilie Le Beau

Lucchesi (2019) highlights an important conclusion made from a study published in *Current Psychology*. He found

> a substantial link between procrastination and clutter problems in all the age groups. Frustration with clutter tended to increase with age. Among older adults, clutter problems were also associated with life dissatisfaction. The findings add to a growing body of evidence that clutter can negatively impact mental well-being, particularly among women. Clutter can also induce a physiological response, including increased levels of cortisol, a stress hormone.

Is it any wonder that rates of teacher burnout and attrition are what they are? If we take these cues from our essentialist and minimalist friends to focus our attention on our purpose, we can more easily align our actions with those intentions. Educator and productivity specialist Angela Watson (2018) reminds us that what we say no to is just as important as what we say yes to. Our real purpose should be equally evident in the things we put our time and effort into, as well as the things we say no to. We need to remove the narrative that we do not have a choice in this matter.

A Mini Historical Lesson on Minimalism

Minimalism originally stems from the principle of nonattachment in Buddhist religious philosophy (O'Brien, 2019), or how attachment to the extraneous things in life can lead to suffering, the foundational First Noble Truth of the Buddhist teachings. This principle is based on achieving joy and enlightenment through detachment, which is sometimes the opposite of what we see and experience in Western industrialized society, yet we see aspects of this cultural belief emerge as part of new approaches to modern lifestyles.

So, when we fast forward to the 1950s and begin to see minimalism popping up in an art movement at the Museum of Modern Art in New York (Glover, 2017), it's a sign that this way of thinking can have a large influence on people's lives, in general.

A Cultural Gap in Minimalism

Historically and culturally, minimalism tends to be represented predominantly in the lifestyles of white Scandinavian and Asian cultures. When thinking of Scandinavia and minimalism, we probably first think of architectural and furniture design. But it goes much deeper than this in traditional culture, as described by the Danish term *hygge* and the Swedish word *lagom*. These terms encapsulate ideals such as life balance, well-being, comfort, and enjoying life and our time. Japanese culture is known for living small, but as explained above, it has deeper roots in Zen Buddhist values in venerating simple lives and rejecting material possessions. Minimalist approaches have more recently been popularly adopted in many countries around the world. Furthermore, we can trace minimalist values to many different religions, philosophers, and leaders around the globe and throughout written history.

However, is this modern experience of minimalism as a lifestyle choice represented equally and similarly across different countries and cultures? The Blackminimalists blog describes that they "experience minimalism differently from the mainstream movement and [they] noticed that [their] voices were not represented on those mainstream minimalist platforms" (Acree, 2017). So perhaps it is reasonable to say that this mainstream approach is less conspicuous or congruous in Black and Brown communities. While we may have read about the reasons behind this and the differences in these experiences outlined in several blogs, we feel that we are not the voices to best convey them. We would, however, like to share the viewpoint of Christine Platt (2020), author and Afrominimalist, who found the spark of beauty in what could be seen as another whitewashed aspect of trending lifestyles by ensuring she did not "let go of her culture just to conform to mainstream minimalism . . . because the beauty and history of the African diaspora are at the core of [her] life's work." Platt went through the decluttering process, a similar process we will be taking you through in this book. Platt also mentions that, for her, minimalism hasn't necessarily been about counting the number of things she owns, but rather having things that serve a purpose in her life and amplify her culture. This is our hope for you as you work through your own process, when you dig into each aspect of teaching in order to find the intentionality in all that takes space in your teaching life.

A Culturally Minded Minimalist Teacher

We recognize that we must remove the historical stigma in a whitewashed education system and dismantle inequities that prevent Black teachers or other educators whose culture may not encapsulate the ideals of minimalism from engaging in a meaningful shift in teaching life. We hope that our framework and questioning translates to educators in schools everywhere at any point in time, shining a light on the positive implications of a minimalist approach to your teaching and learning life. We are a community of individuals who have come from the widest ranges of life experiences, from every culture, from every region of the world, and yet we have all gathered in this one special place: the field of education. We were drawn to this field because we know the importance of learning together and nurturing young minds. We have a desire to affect the communities in which we choose to live, whether near or far from where we were brought up. We hope the minimalist journey provides the benefits of reduced burnout and decreased stress. Maybe the effects will trickle over into your personal life, and maybe not. The key is that you have an entry point here, which can greatly benefit you and your teaching community.

Shifting to a minimalist approach in your teaching life requires you to think deeply about your purpose when educating students. Decluttering does not mean we take away meaning. Decluttering means we find meaning in the essentials, such as shifting our curriculum to become relevant, anti-racist, and as unbiased as possible. It means we shift our instruction and assessment to become trauma-informed and culturally competent.

One path to teach an anti-racist curriculum involves teaching conceptually and removing assessment bias. By removing the clutter of the biased elements of the curriculum and focusing on the students in our classrooms, by learning about who they are and where they have come from, we can design an assessment system *for them*. Statistics show us that year after year, Black students in America are failed by the current standardized assessment structures (Muhammad, 2020). Their scores fall far below the "standard," yet somehow these poorly developed and biased assessments are still used. With this in mind, these assessments can be viewed as a waste of time, money, and energy and can cause a tremendous amount of stress on teachers, students, and their families. Why do we continue to clutter our assessment systems with assessments based on biased information?

However, when teachers can develop conceptual understanding in their anti-racist curriculum, the teaching is honest and the learning is rich. It provides an open space for students to develop insight about how the education system is rooted in racism and layers upon layers of inequities. In her book *Cultivating Genius: An Equity Framework for Culturally and Historically Responsive Literacy,* author and activist Gholdy Muhammad (2020) mentions the use of frameworks that encompass depth, not just skill development. Providing students with unbiased historical information and the space to feel, share, and uncover the system we are all a part of resembles the work that Black organizations have long been doing. It's not a complicated approach, but instead, deep and focused, and it allows for the truth in learning that white students need. It brings concepts such as inequity, social constructs, racism, and activism to the surface and allows for all students to then become equipped to problem solve, think critically, and understand the need to advocate for equity in education for their peers who have been victims of an inequitable system.

For a deeper understanding about the equities that countless BIPOC students face in the education system, we have listed recommended resources by Black educators, as well as a list of Black educators to follow on social media (see Figure I.1). Learn from them throughout this minimalist journey, and focus on the true purpose of education when you pare down to a trauma-sensitive and culturally informed learning experience for your students.

Minimalism in Education

Before we move into a thorough examination of how and why to use our Triple P decision-making questions on page 12, we need to take a moment to consider what should be the springboard for all our work toward decluttering aspects of teaching: research, the fundamental element in school-based decision making. Being mindful of evidence can help prevent us from wasting time, energy, and resources (Sumeracki, Caviglioli, & Weinstein, 2018). Research in education is taking place across many relevant fields, including teaching practices, pedagogy, neuroscience, and cognitive psychology. Why not make use of it? Informed educators need to be able to see through the hyperbole or possible popular trends, and closely examine the research, if any, that supports our ultimate purpose: student learning and growth. Often we see the evidence for initiatives presented in one of two ways:

Figure I.1

BIPOC Educator and Educational Leader Resource List

Sites	• teachingtolerance.org • teachingforchange.org/anti-bias-education • https://www.racialequitytools.org/ • https://www.thebipocproject.org/
Educational leaders to follow	• Dr. Salome Thomas-EL; @principal_EL; http://www.principalel.com/ • Ijeoma Oluo; http://www.ijeomaoluo.com/ and Dr. Ibram Kendi; @DrIbram; https://www.ibramxkendi.com/ • Kevin Simpson; KDSLGlobal and AIELOC; @GlobalKDSL; kdslglobal.com • Craig Martin; @CraigCMartin12; http://craigcmartin.weebly.com/ • Dr. Basil Marin; @basil_marin; basilmarin.com • Cornelius Minor; @MisterMinor; kassandcorn.com • Ki; Woke Kindergarten; @AkieaG • Dr. Paul Gorski; Equity Literacy Institute; @pgorski • Dr. Sheldon Eakins; Leading Equity Center; @sheldoneakins
Writing and talks	• Vernita Mayfield; @DrVMayfield; Cultural Competence Now: 56 Exercises to Help Educators Understand and Challenge Bias, Racism, and Privilege • Bettina Love; @BLoveSoulPower; We Want to Do More Than Survive: Abolitionist Teaching and the Pursuit of Educational Freedom • Gholdy Muhammad; @GholdyM; Cultivating Genius: An Equity Framework for Culturally and Historically Responsive Literacy • Dena Simmons; @DenaSimmons; https://www.denasimmons.com/stockists • Dr. Cheryl Matias; @cheryl_phd; http://www.cherylmatias.com/publications/

1. Research has been undertaken into this exact program or strategy, and here are the positive results. (We followed students in this program, and a control group that wasn't, and here are the benefits for the students who participated.)

2. Aspects of this program or strategy are connected to other research that has been undertaken. And therefore we can assume that our linked approaches will have similar effect sizes. (A group conducted research and found positive effects for *X*. Our program incorporates elements of *X*, and therefore we will probably also have the same impact on learning.)

Additionally, we can consider how the evidence was collected and collated to help us make pertinent decisions. Is the research presented based on empirical evidence or on anecdotal evidence? Have the results been presented in such a way that creates bias in the predicted effectiveness of the program?

Who did the research, and would they have an interest in presenting findings in one way as opposed to another?

Take this example of how research to inform the adoption of initiatives in schools can go awry. Perceptual Motor Programs (PMPs) in Australian schools are physical movement education programs based on the idea that developing perceptual motor skills will support the academic development of young students. They were initially recommended as a remedial support for students or as a whole-school early intervention approach to support young students' development. However, research into the efficacy of actual PMPs showed a close to zero effect size on academic skills and not much more for perceptual motor skills (Stephenson, Carter, & Wheldall, 2007). This research was collated and presented in the 1980s. However, these programs still exist today, with some schools across Australia still using them as both remediation programs and as physical education programs. Stephenson, Carter, and Wheldall discuss the persistence of these programs and suggest that educators are relying on anecdotal success stories, instinct, and easy access to materials over the review and weight of evidence. Teachers are returning to the familiarity and knowledge of this program rather than looking for a more effective but unknown program. Applying our critical thinking skills to the evidence will help us apply our time and efforts to the most effective practices possible. Considering the breadth of all education-based programs, strategies, and tools for learning available, critical thinking should form the foundation on which we build our approach to the decluttering process.

Andrea Felker, a middle school English as an additional language teacher in Singapore, told us that "it would help everyone to be more minimalist. This is a problem—trying to pack far too much into a lesson, trying to use too many different technologies or strategies, schools trying new initiatives because they feel they need to tick a box. Most units are too full, and lessons move too quickly; learning becomes shallower and shallower rather than deeper." Andrea went on to say that many teachers need to be explicitly taught and supported in their efforts to effectively and sustainably create a clutter-free environment. After teaching in a number of schools in several countries in both North America and Asia, she has not taught in a school that has explicitly supported minimalism but rather "schools that value efficiency." She sees this as "a real disadvantage for those who haven't honed their skills in this area, and especially new teachers."

Fortunately, leaders in the minimalist movement have created many different mediums to interact with and support people developing these skills. They have published books, websites, podcasts, documentaries, and TV shows, all focused on their mission to guide people to find meaning in their lives through this lifestyle. Their discussion centers around how the trend toward a life lived through the accumulation of "things" leaves our modern selves feeling adrift, lonely, and purposeless. By reflecting on what is vital in our lives and actively working toward that, we will begin to feel fulfilled and content.

Similarly, if our work in education is made up of the clutter of too many ideas, tasks, initiatives, unnecessary resources, and philosophies, we will also begin to feel lost and overwhelmed. As educators, taking the time to pare down and focus on our priorities will support our greater purpose.

"The Minimalists" discuss the importance of identifying your values, beliefs, or "musts" to free yourself from the extraneous things that are not adding to your life (Millburn & Nicodemus, 2011). Analogously, we have framed the Triple P questions to help you find your priorities and purpose so that you can pare back the unnecessary clutter in your work life and perhaps vice versa. We hope that this will aid you in finding your impetus and satisfaction in your role as an educator.

Counterintuitively to this work, the media, and what seems to be the whole of society, bombards us with the idea that more is better. We must realize that this is not so. We also need to understand that in our process to find purpose, prioritize, and pare down, we must undo prior learning that has developed habits of wanting more or thinking you need more. At this point, we have Prochaska and DiClemente (1983) to thank for their theory about these behaviors. As a result, they developed the transtheoretical model, "an integrative, biopsychosocial model to conceptualize the process of intentional behavior change." The model outlines the "stages of change" to describe how people approach and conquer change. By choosing to read our book, you have already passed the precontemplation stage, in which people are not quite ready to acknowledge they need help and do not have any intention of making change in the next six months. You, on the other hand, are likely further along in the contemplation stage (ready to change in the coming months), the preparation stage (ready now), the action stage (you have already started making changes in recent months), or the maintenance stage (working to prevent relapse). For whichever stage you identify, we have a set of tools for you.

Introducing the Triple P Framework

Throughout the book, we will be working through the different elements of the overall Triple P framework. The whole framework includes the overarching Triple P questions, the Triple P funnel and decision-making questions to focus priorities, and the Triple P cycle. Let's look at each of these elements now.

Triple P Decision Making

When discussing ideas for this book, we knew introducing new educational jargon or acronyms that did not meet the goal of transforming to a minimalist approach would be a poor decision. Yet, we knew we needed a simple phrase that *would* stick in a cluttered teacher's mind to move the work ahead. After we boiled down many of our professional conversations, as well as conversations we have had about writing this book, we were consistently coming back to three main points resulting in what we have called the Triple P questions part of our Triple P framework.

1. What is our purpose?
2. What are our priorities?
3. How can we pare down resources?

Purpose: Every day we ask ourselves easy-to-answer questions. "Why am I running when my knee hurts?" Easy answer. "Why am I using this product instead of that one?" Easy again. But when we ask ourselves, "Why would I teach that?" or, "Why would I teach that in this way?" we must peel back the layers of teaching and learning, because there are so many "Why am I doing this?" questions to ask.

Priority: Now, here lies a great challenge. How do you prioritize when there are just so many "things" that require attention? Go back to your purpose to help you build your prioritization muscles. Your priority will always be the well-being and learning experiences of your students. Always and forever. Remember this when your mind is swamped because we know from experience that our priorities are masked by other clutter. In schools, items for discussions are usually prioritized by time and money, not by student or teacher needs. How do you unmask these mandated compliance tasks in a short time frame while still ensuring integrity in your teaching and, quite honestly, your sanity? While the Triple P questions become more intricate when peeling back the layers, remain simple in your response: your students are your priority.

Pare Down: Last but certainly not least—how does one pare down all that "stuff" so that priorities match purposes? How do you really do more with less? This may become the most challenging part of the transformation of practice. The challenge comes with letting go of things, control, and feeling overwhelmed to make space for increased efficiency, productivity, and new feelings of satisfaction and supported well-being. We will work with you through this process of letting go.

Throughout each chapter of this book, we will examine various ways in which Triple P decision making will guide you in finding solutions and making improvements in your work. Unfortunately, we could not write a book about a minimalist approach and address every aspect of teaching. That would result in a book hundreds of pages too long! However, our hope is that Triple P is open-ended enough for you to refer back and find your way to solutions in almost any area of teaching. Whether it is working with parents, using hours of your free time to plan, navigating team collaboration meetings, or putting together portfolios, considering your purpose, priorities, and how to pare down will help you find a navigable way through the clutter. To support your work ahead, we have included Appendix B, which has nonexhaustive lists of initiatives, purposes, and priorities for each chapter of the book.

The Triple P Funnel

To help you visualize how the Triple P decision-making process flows, imagine a funnel like in Figure I.2. A funnel allows you to pour a large amount of substance through the open top. As it moves through the funnel, the substance passes through a narrower area, finally filtering into your intended space. That space at the bottom of your funnel is where you create intentionality in each element of your teaching life. The process of funneling is careful and deliberate. We sift through our workload to ensure extraneous or oversized elements do not end up in our filtered result. As you work through your questioning and decision making, you are filtering and sifting for the essential elements only, not removing the important pieces, only the extraneous distractors, blockers, and space fillers.

Figure I.2
The Triple P Funnel

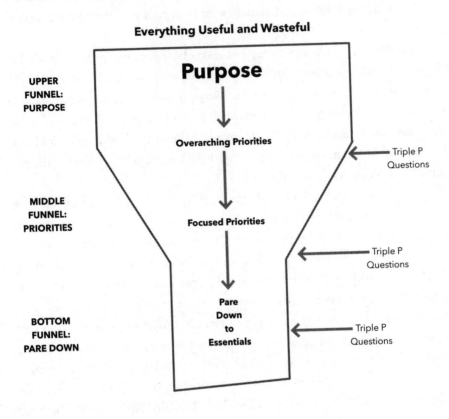

- **Top Funnel.** This is the place where all forms of everything useful and wasteful (time, energy, money, mental and intellectual effort) coexist, just before we dump everything into the funnel.
- **Upper Funnel.** This is the place where we look at all the elements and determine the overarching purpose before we start to filter all the pieces more carefully. Determining your overarching purpose or goal will allow you to clarify the supporting priorities. At this funnel level, we ask, "What is our main purpose here?"
- **Middle Funnel.** Once your purpose is clear, you will begin asking yourself some more Triple P questions as you filter into the middle funnel. Here you will ask, "What is our main priority or couple of priorities that will support our purpose?"

- **Bottom Funnel.** As you sort out your priorities and your elements are becoming clearer, at this point you can ask more specific questions around your priorities such as "What is the priority in this element for this class, student, or teacher?"

The Triple P Cycle

Now that you have been introduced to our Triple P framework and have seen the fundamental elements of finding your purpose, priorities, and how to pare down—and how the Triple P funnel allows you to narrow your focus— you may also begin to notice a series of events taking shape. As we work through the necessary changes toward becoming more minimalist in our approach to education, you will notice a series of repeated experiences form that will take us through the process of the Triple P cycle in Figure I.3.

Figure I.3
The Triple P Cycle

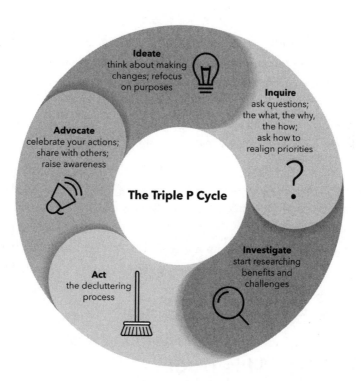

As you move through the chapters and utilize the entire Triple P frame-work (funnel, cycle, and questions), you will begin to see that you are going through a process of considering new ideas, asking questions, and investigating benefits and challenges in your own context before moving into taking action (description in Appendix A). We encourage you to complete this cycle by advocating to those around you about what you have discovered and found successful.

The Cycle Element for Introductory Ideas

Ideate. This introduction has you at the ideation phase of the cycle. You are thinking about making changes in practice and want to refocus on the greater *purpose* of teaching. This is extremely important to recognize as you take on new thinking and create new habits within your practice.

To assist you in being mindful about your own individual process and journey, we have included markers throughout the chapters to remind you what stage you are working in and where you will be moving next. Our hope is that this will prompt you to be considerate of where you are to deepen the engagement and deliberation throughout your participation. If you find yourself taking action before you've had a chance to really inquire and investigate, you know that you may not be making the most informed decisions. If you miss a step, go back to previous markers and reread to ensure you are truly considering your purpose and priorities before taking any next steps.

When Pam was trying to convince herself not to attend art school on an episode of the American version of *The Office,* Jan told her that "[t]here are always a million reasons not to do something." You may be thinking of your million reasons not to take on this transformation as you read this chapter, but we ask you to think of all the reasons you should.

How to Use This Book

Before reading the rest of the book, ask yourself the following questions:

- Do you think you could develop a stronger sense of community and purpose in your classroom?

- Do you store resources that have been sitting in your room unused?
- Are you avoiding your administrative team because you know they will ask you to do something else?
- Do you teach a curriculum that is overwhelmingly overloaded?
- Does planning rich learning experiences cause you to feel overwhelmed?
- Are your assessment practices scattered and not as useful as they could be?
- Are you unsure about how to move ahead with speaking up for a better system of teaching and learning in your classroom?

Have one or more of the questions got you nodding your head with a little too much vigor? Well, good news then, because we have written *The Minimalist Teacher* with the intent that educators can choose to read the chapters about their specific decluttering needs, or as a whole. We do recommend reading Chapter 1 to set the stage for understanding the purpose of decluttering and then moving on to any chapter based on the desired topic. The book is not intended to be read in order, but it can be.

Once you have answered these questions, you can determine how you will read the book. Figure I.4 provides a couple of suggestions to help enhance your experience.

Chapter Summaries

Merely thinking about the work ahead might be daunting, uncomfortable, and exhausting. It may cause some anxiety and worry, but to create space by weeding through the clutter is an essential step in helping you clearly focus on the purpose in your practice. To reduce mental fatigue and support choosing your starting point, we have provided chapter summaries for this book.

Chapter 1: Creating a Culture of Minimalism in Your Classroom highlights the importance of creating a culture of minimalism by establishing a shared understanding of what minimalist teaching and learning can represent in classrooms. We highlight and discover our priorities in creating a culture of minimalism and establish protocols for how to create it by developing knowledge, habits, and relevance.

Chapter 2: Decluttering the Physical Environment examines the perils of waste that partner with having a classroom. Further, we explore tools for

Figure I.4

Suggested Uses for the Book

Suggested Use	Process and Actions
Reading on your own	1. Answer the above reflection questions. 2. Determine your professional need from your responses to the questions above. 3. Take your time to read the target chapter and use its tools for reflection to guide you in the process of decluttering. 4. Share the process with your colleagues (the feedback loop is crucial in the sustainability of this practice). 5. Support another colleague with the same problem of practice. 6. Share your successes and challenges with us via Twitter using #MinimalistTeacher. 7. Use the cycle as a reminder to continue your new habits.
Reading with a professional learning community (PLC)	1. Answer the above reflection questions independently, then share responses with the PLC. 2. Determine your problem of practice. 3. Group with like response colleagues or work as a whole group. 4. Schedule meetings with your group to determine how you will read, document reflections, and share the process. 5. Take your time to read the target chapter and use its tools for reflection to guide you and your PLC in the process of decluttering. 6. Visit one another's classrooms where appropriate to make observations and provide thoughtful feedback on progress. 7. Meet consistently with your PLC, as the feedback loop is crucial in the sustainability of this practice. Ensure other meetings or events take precedence over your sessions. 8. Share your successes and challenges with us via Twitter using #MinimalistTeacher. 9. Continue to check in with your PLC group, even when your scheduled times are completed or you have finished reading the chapter or book, by using the Triple P funnel in your future meetings.

Reading with a professional book club	1. Survey colleagues to gauge interest in starting a professional book club (if not already in place).
	2. Plan out if you will discuss by chapter or after reading the entire book. In either case, determine your method of discussion, and determine your "read by" date.
	3. Use the book study questions in Appendix C as a guide.
	4. Upon completion of the book, meet in a social setting to have a final discussion about your reflections and takeaways, and be prepared to share your action plans.
	5. Continue to check in with your book club members to keep a clear reflection and feedback cycle rolling for sustainability of practices.
	6. Share your successes and challenges with us via Twitter using #MinimalistTeacher.
	7. Continue to use the Triple P framework and funnel to continue your new decision-making process and/or use the cycle to continue your new habits.

evaluating the quality and purpose of physical resources along with tips for paring them down and maximizing each part of a physical classroom space.

Chapter 3: Decluttering Initiatives explains the importance of a teacher's voice in the process of decluttering school-based initiatives. While many teachers will feel decluttering initiatives fall in the role of school administrators, administration teams sometimes use a model of distributive leadership and building teacher capacity. This model brings teacher teams together to be involved in the process of decluttering initiatives that are funneled down from states and districts. This chapter provides reflection questions and thinking charts to develop purpose, priorities, and ways to pare down both large-scale and school-based initiatives.

Chapter 4: Decluttering the Curriculum digs deeper into the intellectual and time waste that teachers face when confronted with curriculum choice. In this chapter, we dig into what curriculum is and how to weed through the extraneous pieces. The chapter is full of ideas to support strengthening your curriculum with richer support and plenty of practical tips to pare down process so that chosen resources are best suited for efficiency in planning and enhanced learning.

Chapter 5: Decluttering Instructional and Assessment Strategies digs into the real purpose of your instruction and the role of assessment within it. Find what's best for your practices by brainstorming priorities and identifying which are specific to your purpose. We unpack strategies and practical ideas to combat the time waste issue all teachers face during instructional and assessment time. This chapter provides research-based routines and strategies that will provide more "bounce for your ounce" and will help alleviate planning stress.

Chapter 6: Advocating for Minimalism in Your Teaching Environment provides insight into how the Triple P process can rewire detrimental waste into an overall positive experience in school. Benefits of advocating for a minimalist approach to teaching are explored, and practical tools are examined, including an advocacy audit and action plan.

Appendices: We have put together some lists and additional tools to support each step of the cycle and Triple P questioning. You will find the following:

- Appendix A: The Triple P Cycle
- Appendix B: Initiatives, Purposes, and Priorities
- Appendix C: The Minimalist Teacher Book Study Guide

In Conclusion

Chapter Takeaway

Our goal is to support all educators, and ultimately their students, to find the mental space to declutter your crowded role and eventually work through the Triple P decision-making process organically. This process will seep into your work with students and ultimately into the school community. It will allow you to foster awareness of minimalism as a part of classroom and school culture and teach deep learning without all the extra "stuff." This is a practice that all members of any school community can advocate for when the purpose and benefits are clear.

Lingering Question

Where do I need to begin my process?

Up Next

We suggest you spend time working through the first chapter in this book. We'll take you through key ideas about a minimalist culture and tips for getting yourself and your students ready for your minimalist classroom environment. Good luck and enjoy the journey ahead.

Creating a Culture of Minimalism in Your Classroom

The Purpose for Creating a Culture of Minimalism in Your Classroom

The term "culture" can bring to mind a variety of different images or meanings. This can encompass anything from language or food to the arts or family structures. Ultimately, a culture is a shared set of values and practices that are held by a group of people. A culture of minimalism requires members of a group, in this case your classroom, to recognize and work toward making use of currently available resources and no *more* in order to best support the requirements and expectations of the community. While a minimalist culture in classrooms may seem unconventional, overly innovative, or unrealistic now, this approach is becoming more and more socially acceptable. Rather than superficially attempting to meet students' needs by buying "things," adding more tasks, or creating more paperwork, there is a shift to instead maximize existing resources in the community and create a lifelong practice and lifestyle of appreciation, efficiency, and sustainability.

At this point, we do not need to use the Triple P funnel because the process to establish classroom culture is different from how to declutter the elements of your teaching. However, as we begin unpacking priorities in creating a culture of minimalism in your classroom, and really your teaching life, we can correlate two stages in the cycle. During this time, you are working in the *inquiry* and *investigation* phases of the cycle, moving you further on with your investigation.

The Cycle Elements for Creating the Culture

? **Inquire.** In this phase, ask yourself and others about *priorities* in teaching and learning, including the what, why, and how of shifting practice.

Q **Investigate.** This phase gets you to research, read, and understand the benefits and challenges of a minimalism approach, including why others go through this process and why it is a *priority* for you.

Priorities in Creating This Culture

When you recognize the purpose of creating a minimalist culture in your classroom—to create a mindset of efficiency and appreciation and practice it—priorities become clearer and simpler to address. Below, we've highlighted three main priorities to answer why you might wish to develop this mindset within your classroom contexts.

Priority #1: Positive well-being and avoiding burnout

Anyone in education, in any capacity, can attest to the fact that it is exhausting. Research studies about teacher burnout have been consistent in their findings across Africa, Asia, Australia, Canada, Europe, the Middle East, New Zealand, and South America.

In her article "The Teacher Burnout Epidemic, Part 1 of 2," Jenny Grant Rankin (2016) states that, while teacher workloads are different world-wide, they are at a maximum. In 2014, reports showed that 8 percent of all American teachers were leaving the field each year. Of those leaving, a 2012–2013 teacher survey by the National Center for Education Statistics (Goldring, Taie, & Riddles, 2014) reported more than half said their new profession's workload was significantly lower than when they were working as teachers. In addition to that, a 2019 National Foundation for Educational Research (NFER) report highlights that teachers are consistently reporting more stress than those in alternative professions. Finally, a resounding 41 percent of teachers leave the profession in their first five years, highlighting a workforce quitting before they have had the opportunity to truly master skills and take their profession to the next level, according to Dr. Jenny Grant Rankin (2016).

Clearly our chosen profession is one in which our well-being and mental health are at risk. These pressures may be coming from a wide range of causes: federal mandates, administration/districts, parent population, accountability standards, or the students themselves. But wherever they may be coming from, we are *all* feeling it.

Our hope is that through developing a minimalist culture within your work environment, you will be able to reduce the level of exhaustion you feel. Ideally, focusing on your purpose, priorities, and ways to pare down will allow you to have the emotional and intellectual energy to continue in this valuable profession.

Priority #2: Reconceptualizing waste in order to combat waste

When we think about minimalism and waste, we of course consider the extraneous items that clutter our room. We think of what we can get rid of and how to dispose of all those unnecessary items. However, in order to reset our mindset toward a culture of minimalism, we need to expand our thinking around what actually constitutes waste. A broader understanding of waste will help shift the way we approach how we work and function in our working environments, such as the many different facets of waste that can occur: time, emotional, intellectual and psychological (mental), economic, and physical or resource waste. Each day in our work as teachers we could encounter waste in any, or all, of these ways, leaving us feeling stressed, ineffective, and anxious. Consider the following examples:

- **Time waste:** Planning lessons that require excessive time and preparation.
- **Emotional/psychological waste:** Taking feedback from administration or parents personally.
- **Economic waste:** Repurchasing items you already have but have misplaced in the clutter of the classroom.
- **Physical waste:** Filling every space of the classroom until it no longer functions effectively.

Reconceptualizing waste in this way will allow you to combat waste in a less superficial manner and really build a culture of minimalism in your classroom. When we have extraneous clutter in our lives, be it abstract or physical things, we are overcome with waste. This idea is counterproductive to your priority to prevent burnout. When we focus on the purpose, priority, and paring down process, we can reduce all the different kinds of waste.

Priority #3: Managing waste beyond the four Rs

In *Less Stuff*, Lindsay Miles (2019) discusses the importance of considering what will happen to our physical clutter when we are done with it. She argues that we need to think sustainably and move beyond just shifting our unwanted clutter to a landfill. Other potential ways to remedy a growing waste concern is to consider reusing, repurposing, repairing, and recycling.

Waste reduction helps create a culture of minimalism and reduce potential burnout. Consider the following questions:

- If we cannot reuse items ourselves, is there someone else who might find a use, whether for its intended or an adapted purpose?
- Is it possible to repair the items if they are not in use due to damage?
- Could the item, or its components, be recycled?

What Are Your Priorities?

Now that we have highlighted both the purpose and priorities of establishing a classroom culture of minimalism, we encourage you to consider your own priorities moving forward. To do this, let's use the urgent/important matrix in Figure 1.1. Plot the following elements on the matrix, and you will quickly establish which are of critical importance for you to take action on at this time.

Where would you place the following on the matrix?

- Maintenance or restoration of your well-being
- Avoiding burnout
- Minimizing time waste
- Minimizing emotional/psychological waste
- Minimizing economic waste
- Minimizing physical waste
- Sustainably managing waste

Figure 1.1
Urgent/Important Matrix

	Urgent	Not so urgent
Important	High priority: Take action immediately	Medium priority: Make a plan
Not so important	Medium priority: Make a plan	Neither urgent nor important: Eliminate as a priority

What did you discover? Do you urgently need to take action to prevent burnout? Or is economic waste a more important priority for you at this time? Now armed with a definitive vision of where you need to take action, we can begin our discussion about just *how* to go about creating this culture.

How to Create a Minimalist Classroom Culture

To develop a culture of minimalism in your classroom that is sustainable for you and your students, we have identified three areas that can support this work: developing knowledge, examining expectations and opportunities through routines and habits, and understanding relevance. These three main facets will form the core of how to positively shift the culture of your classroom in order to meet your priorities.

1. Developing the Knowledge to Build an Understanding About Minimalism

To begin the physical work of creating a minimalist classroom environment, all classroom community members will need to build their knowledge beyond just cleaning and recycling. One way to do that is to develop a mindset that focuses on the benefits of paring down the physical environment and how clutter can affect well-being. Figure 1.2 provides several resources to help you handle different types of waste. If you and your students already have some understanding of how to identify waste and how it contributes to burnout and overload, you can provide families with tools for understanding, too. You can help them understand why embarking on this journey to create less waste and use resources more thoughtfully will benefit their school learning environments as well as their families at home.

Figure 1.2

Resources to Build Knowledge and Develop Understanding of Minimalist Culture

Waste Type	Resources	How It Builds Knowledge
Time	Article: National Education Organization, "Time Management Tips for Educators" https://bit.ly/3jRpU7w	• Strategies for effective time management from planning to teaching.
	Article: *New York Times*, "Productivity Isn't About Time Management. It's Attention Management" https://nyti.ms/37hy7Nu	• Insight into how we manage our attention relates to our use of time.
	Picture Book: *See You Later Procrastinator (Get It Done)* by Pamela Espeland and Elizabeth Verdick https://amzn.to/3aliDK4	• Easy-to-read tips, stories, and strategies to assist students in making the best use of their time.

Emotional and Psychological	Article: *Psychology Today,* "How to Take Feedback" https://bit.ly/3doFPJg	• Insight into the negative emotions associated with criticism. • Eight rules for effective feedback.
	Book: *The Book of Overthinking: How to Stop the Cycle of Worrying* by Gwendoline Smith https://amzn.to/3u4KMNI	• Insight into the positives and negative related to overthinking.
	Picture Book: *Ruby's Worry* by Tom Percival https://amzn.to/2NaBwGP	• Read-aloud activities to support students managing worries.
	Book: *No Worries! Mindful Kids: An Activity Book for Children Who Sometimes Feel Anxious or Stressed* by Dr. Sharie Coombs https://bit.ly/3tW1fnb	
Economic and Physical	Site: "The Story of Stuff" http://thestoryofstuff.org	• Solid foundation for building an understanding of systems thinking and how using less will benefit us all. • A systemic approach of how humans contribute to the development of waste.
	Picture Book: *Too Many Toys* by David Shannon https://amzn.to/3u1KRBz Picture Book: *What a Waste* by Jess French https://amzn.to/37jbt7f Book: *Trash Revolution: Breaking the Waste Cycle* by Erica Fyvie https://amzn.to/3dggl0F	• Engaging read-aloud or book club books to open discussions about physical waste.
	Site: Environmental Protection Agency's "The Quest for Less" https://bit.ly/37zpxdd	• Resources, curricula, and lessons for students in K–8 to learn about waste management and reduction.

2. Expectations and Opportunities: Establishing Routines and Habits

We have established that when creating a culture around a concept, particularly a new concept, we must understand it is about changing mindsets and developing new knowledge. But we also need to recognize that in this process we need to create new habits in which a community of students, families, and school staff can see the value of these new changes. In his book *Simplicity*, Edward de Bono (2015) states that "the human brain tries its hardest to simplify life by setting up routine patterns of perception and action. Once you identify the flow of pattern, you flow along without further effort" (p. 18).

Ron Ritchhart (2015) describes several ways in which we can build an informed classroom culture, without adding material things, initiatives, or programs to the pile of clutter. He discusses eight cultural forces: expectations, language, time, modeling opportunities, routines, interactions, and environment. Simply looking through the list of cultural forces should be encouraging. Why? Because these are likely elements of building your classroom culture that you are already doing. The key here is to focus on the deliberate development of these cultural forces. From our perspective, we can likely pare this down even more by creating two broader categories: expectations and opportunities.

Building the culture of minimalism is intentional and straightforward yet brilliantly rich and full. Lisa Fort, a high school earth science teacher in Queensbury, New York, told us that "the value is in having a vision for classroom efficiency, which then translates to the needs [and] materials to make a classroom run within those expectations." To this end, Figures 1.3 and 1.4 provide a deconstruction of expectations and opportunities in a way that will allow you to see the connection between Ritchhart's eight cultural forces and our stripped-down approach to creating a minimalist culture in your classroom.

3. Make It Relevant

Approaching teaching and learning through the lens of "doing less with more," as we have previously outlined, is very timely and relevant to current social mindsets. Our ideas to support the decluttering process in our own spaces while developing responsible consumption with students are the focus of a larger movement. When we do this work in our daily lives with our students, we work toward meeting the United Nations Sustainable

Figure 1.3

Expectations in a Minimalist Classroom Culture

Expectations: A clear standard for behaviors and words used in learning environments	
How Teachers Can Set Expectations	Classroom Examples
Intentional use of language with students supports a "needs vs. wants" culture.	"We need new . . ." vs. "We are running out of . . . so make sure we use . . . thoughtfully."
Use language that supports the knowledge and skills needed to develop this understanding of minimalism in the classroom.	"I like that you used both sides of your paper." vs. "You have used your resources carefully."
Model thoughtful actions that support intentional use of items or interactions with people.	Reuse items, such as containers for storage. Remove a trash bin from the classroom and replace it with different recycle bins and compost collection bins.
Model thoughtful actions that support intentional interactions with others.	Raise awareness to student actions of intention, such as using resources thoughtfully or bringing in items from home for use. Raise awareness to students when interactions among them support the culture of "need vs. want."
Plan learning experiences that help students understand that learning is a process and requires intentional use of time rather than a distraction of "unnecessities."	"We only have 10 minutes for this." vs. "We will be working on . . . for the next few days so that we can understand. . . ."
Use clear communication that the environment is a learning tool for all members of the community.	Set up the classroom environment intentionally for ease of movement and flow between activities and areas. Carefully choose physical resources and furniture for communal use, multipurpose activities, comfort, and a sense of calm. All parties are responsible for ensuring that materials are replaced when finished to make it easy for the next person.

Figure 1.4

Opportunities in a Minimalist Classroom Culture

Teacher Action	Examples of Intentional Learning Opportunities That Support Development of Minimalist Culture
Planned Learning Opportunities	Physical copies of paper are minimal or nonexistent. Materials are prepared with communal use in mind, such as one chart paper for a group of students or a dedicated notebook or digital folder for student work. Resources are gathered with the intent that students will independently identify if they need more.
Learning Time	Instructional time is short and targeted. Content instruction is deliberate.
Routines	Classroom routines are intentionally introduced and consistently practiced to reinforce good use of time and resources. Respond to needs in the room. For example, "We don't have enough glue sticks for everyone in the room. What habit can we establish to share these resources?"
Language and Interactions That Build Awareness	Engage in impromptu conversations around minimalism and our role in working toward it. Model how to interact with others positively when discussing possibly triggering topics.

Development Goals, or SDGs (https://sdgs.un.org/goals), which were developed as a 17-point plan to achieve worldwide prosperity and peace by 2030. This plan was adopted by all members of the UN in 2015. As such, it is extremely crucial, timely, and relevant to make connections for ourselves and students to the work we are doing to minimize in this way. We can teach our students that purpose, priorities, and paring down are beneficial beyond ourselves and also help the broader community.

Minimalist Classroom Culture Audit

As was stated earlier, the forces that create culture are most likely elements that you are already actively doing in your classroom. But how focused are your practices in creating a culture of minimalism specifically? What do you need to inquire about or investigate? Have a read through the minimalist classroom culture audit in Figure 1.5 to help you consider where you currently are in creating a minimalist culture within your classroom. Simply check off each statement to highlight the areas you are already doing and where you may need to move next.

Figure 1.5

Minimalist Classroom Culture Audit

Already Do	Creating a Minimalist Culture in My Classroom	To Do
MINDSET AND KNOWLEDGE		
☐	I have a personal understanding of a minimalist culture and its benefits for my classroom community.	☐
☐	My students have an understanding of a minimalist culture and its benefits for our classroom community.	☐
☐	My students' parents and caregivers have an understanding of a minimalist culture and its benefits for our classroom community.	☐
☐	We have conversations about our practices and are consistently working toward keeping our physical and psychological spaces clutter-free.	☐
☐	I have shared family-friendly resources to help my students and their families learn more about a culture of minimalism and its benefits in the classroom environment.	☐
ROUTINES AND HABITS		
☐	We have established expectations that support us to use only what we need to enhance learning.	☐
☐	I consistently model intentional action, language use, and thoughtful interaction.	☐

continued

Figure 1.5 (*continued*)
Minimalist Classroom Culture Audit

	ROUTINES AND HABITS	
☐	We use our time as efficiently as possible. We spend time on experiences that add value rather than on distractions or time-fillers.	☐
☐	I give recognition to students who demonstrate independence or efforts toward creating habits of minimalism.	☐
☐	Our language reflects thoughtful resource use and interaction consistently.	☐
☐	Students provide each other with support and reminders to act intentionally and make best use of time, energy, and resources.	☐
	RELEVANCE	
☐	Students have an understanding of the connections between our own actions and sustainable lifestyles.	☐
☐	Students feel empowered to use their understanding of a culture of minimalism in other areas of the school community and beyond.	☐
☐	Students feel empowered to take ownership of the culture created in the classroom by sharing practices at home.	☐

Now:

1. Choose three of your to-dos from the above checklist and begin thinking through it.

2. Consider how these fit within your priorities based on what you now know about creating a culture of minimalism in your classroom.

In Conclusion

Chapter Takeaways

- There are three main priorities in developing a minimalist culture:
  - Positive well-being and avoiding burnout
  - Reconceptualizing waste in order to combat waste
  - Managing waste beyond the four Rs
- A culture of minimalism requires developing knowledge, establishing routines, and understanding life relevance.
- Consider your own priorities and the steps you can take to build culture.

Lingering Question

I see why creating the culture of minimalism in my classroom is important, but how can I be sure others will see the importance, too?

Up Next

Are you ready to dive in? If you are moving straight into Chapter 2: Decluttering the Physical Environment, we are getting right into all the physical and mental decluttering. In Chapter 2 we focus on evaluating the utility of your classroom by identifying the purpose and priorities associated with each area of the room. It's a thought-provoking process that can spark some emotions. This chapter will support you in reflecting on what you already have in the room and how you can make the best use of all it contains. Get ready for some decluttering!

Decluttering the Physical Environment

The Problem: Cluttered Classroom Spaces

Classroom environments become cluttered with "unnecessities" masked as necessities. In reality, many of these items are nothing more than economic and resource waste. Teachers all over the world suffer from clutter fatigue. Many colleagues have shared that they dread moving into new spaces for fear that they will be clearing out years of accumulated teacher clutter.

Part of teacher conditioning is also to get caught in the trap of collecting resources and holding on to them indefinitely. We write on sticky notes to remember something and then end up with sticky notes everywhere, not remembering what the shorthand referenced in the first place. We become experts at finding games at garage sales to enhance learning. Or we add items like inspirational quote posters to our wish lists in order to motivate learners. Teacher store catalogs alone can clutter a classroom shelf. Store carts and online shopping baskets get filled with attractive items and entice teachers into thinking the kids need it. It is beautiful *and* standards-based! Realistically, we know these things will end up in our cupboards, used once or twice, unless we make a point of intentionally keeping less, resulting in greater use of the fewer items we do keep.

Now, we would never tell a teacher to refrain from purchasing some fantastic games or exciting new manipulatives for their students. What we do want to say is that you can purchase new resources and have the space for them, but only after you have systematically evaluated your existing ones. This chapter is about reflecting on your classroom and finding purpose in what you already have, prioritizing how to use it, and paring down "unnecessities."

The Cycle Elements for the Physical Environment

Act. This *paring-down* process will take a good chunk of your time and energy, as it focuses not only on the physical decluttering but also how you feel when you are in the process.

*Note: You will likely find yourself working through multiple phases in the cycle. You may Inquire and Investigate to gather more ideas and research about space use.

What Am I Decluttering from My Classroom?

Don't Get Rid of Everything

Often when we read about the movement toward minimalism, we encounter boundaries or quantifiers of some sort or another:

- "This person only owns 50 possessions."
- "Declutter your home in 25 days."

- "Tips to live a zero-waste, minimalist lifestyle."
- "Travel the world with only a carry-on bag."
- "Forty things to stop buying."
- "Use the 50/20/30 rule for a minimalist budget."

On and on the systems, challenges, and gauges go. But behind each system, there is a similar intention: to move your life toward one that is more fulfilling and less about the "stuff" that surrounds us.

How can we translate this action into a classroom context? Are we about to advocate throwing out everything in your classroom to become a minimalist teacher? Do we recommend a magic number of resources to keep on your shelves? Do we have a standard set of steps that will work for every teacher in every school? Absolutely not. Minimalism in the physical environment is about prioritizing, finding the purpose, and paring down to the essentials to act with intention in the classroom.

Caution: Scarcity Mindset

Too frequently in schools, we wind up lacking resources or funding for student essentials. Whether it is a lack of teachers, teaching spaces, teaching materials, or paper, we have probably all experienced scarcity in schools to some extent. When we have experienced this lack of critical resources, it can lead to a scarcity mindset, the psychological effect of not having enough to meet a need, which then becomes an overwhelming and focused concern that scarcity may continue indefinitely. In the school context, this can result in holding on to every possible resource, just on the off chance that it may be necessary in the future. It becomes too much of a comfort to hold on to every scrap of wrapping paper, 20-year-old magazine, take-out container, and broken game because you never know when it might come in handy. The end result? Cluttered, heaving classrooms. Classrooms packed with much junk and very little value. It is time to move beyond this mindset.

Why Am I Decluttering My Classroom?

Creating Calm Through Decluttering

Lindsay Miles discusses how extraneous clutter leaves us feeling unwanted stress and reduces our productivity and efficacy in her book *Less Stuff* (2019). She outlines how getting rid of extra objects and mess in our physical spaces leaves us feeling calmer and more comfortable to get on with what we need to be doing. Additionally, our brains need time to process all the clutter in a room, so if our eyes are visually processing everything every time we enter a room, imagine the amount of stress a cluttered space creates for a child's brain. Reducing the clutter creates calm (Gonzalez, 2018). Kristine Miller, a teacher in Virginia, agrees, adding that reducing the amount of clutter would probably alleviate some of the stress.

Now, turn your attention to tackling this task within your own classroom. We know that making an effort to declutter will lead us to feel more purposeful, calm, and comfortable. We are also aware that consciously moving away from solely viewing items in our rooms through a scarcity mindset will allow us to act with intention in our working spaces.

Triple P Funneling

Come with us as we take the first few steps forward in moving toward a decluttered, calm space, filled only with the actual necessities, by guiding you through the Triple P funnel with some questions.

In the 1980s movie *The Karate Kid*, Daniel said he "never had karate training like this before; sure wish I knew how it worked." You may have the same sentiment as you stand and look at your classroom space because in your physical space, every type of clutter exists—physical, economic, mental, intellectual. Seeing clutter has a proven negative impact on mental clarity. This is the place where we recognize all the elements of the space, useful and otherwise.

By recognizing all the kinds of waste, you will begin to think about the overarching purpose of your physical space. Even though we are evaluating the physical space, you must also think about the social and intellectual use of the space to ensure your purpose becomes clear. As you begin asking yourself some Triple P questions, you will begin to filter through both the purpose and priorities within each space and the purpose for the materials within them.

At this point you begin to zone in on specific resources and determine the true value they add to the learning space. This can be an emotional journey because there may be stockpiles of items or mementos from your previous years of teaching, but you need to ask yourself, "What items can I subtract without diminishing the value of the room and its areas? What are

Figure 2.1

Environment Triple P Questions and Decision Making

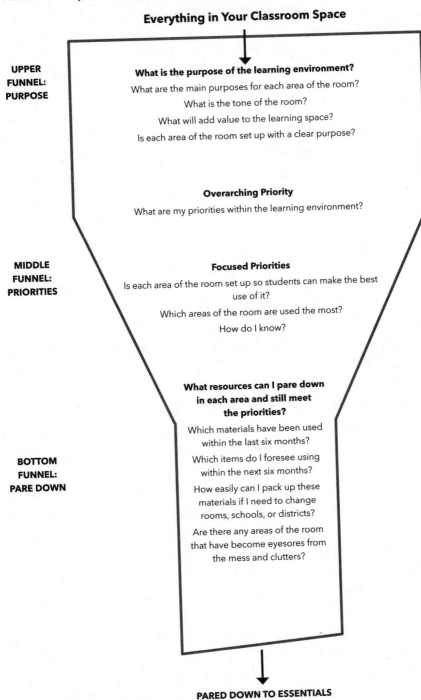

Everything in Your Classroom Space

UPPER FUNNEL: PURPOSE

What is the purpose of the learning environment?

What are the main purposes for each area of the room?

What is the tone of the room?

What will add value to the learning space?

Is each area of the room set up with a clear purpose?

Overarching Priority

What are my priorities within the learning environment?

MIDDLE FUNNEL: PRIORITIES

Focused Priorities

Is each area of the room set up so students can make the best use of it?

Which areas of the room are used the most?

How do I know?

What resources can I pare down in each area and still meet the priorities?

Which materials have been used within the last six months?

Which items do I foresee using within the next six months?

How easily can I pack up these materials if I need to change rooms, schools, or districts?

Are there any areas of the room that have become eyesores from the mess and clutters?

BOTTOM FUNNEL: PARE DOWN

PARED DOWN TO ESSENTIALS

the items I can keep that add value to learning and can be used for multiple purposes?" Working through the upper funnel questions will help you mentally prepare for the physical decluttering ahead. Use Figure 2.1 as a guide.

Let the Decluttering Begin!

Step 1

Think purposefully about your classroom space. The first step in this process is to lay a critical, objective eye across the various areas that make up your room. Take a moment to inventory the spaces you have in your classroom. Below is a list of reasonably common classroom spaces:

- White/black/interactive board
- Mat or rug area
- Classroom library
- Desk area
- Bulletin boards
- Window area
- Shelving

Step 2

Once you have written your list of spaces, we are going to pause to reflect on what the purpose is for each space or category, like in Figure 2.2. Consider each space beyond the area it takes up; think about what purpose it currently serves or perhaps what purpose you would like it to serve. For example, what is the true intention of including that space in your room?

Figure 2.2
Example Classroom Spaces Assessment

Space/Category	What Is the Purpose?
Central consumable materials storage shelf or cart	• Classroom community use • Accessible to all learners
Mat area or central gathering area	• Student interactions • Student access to materials to support learning • Space to encourage frequent reading or game playing to enhance literacy or math skills

Step 3

Write down what considerations or materials are the main priority for each space to meet its purpose. What does each area need for it to fulfill the intention? It may be a physical object, or it may be a more conceptual inclusion such as safety or accessibility. To provide you with a clear vision of what this process can look like, Figure 2.3 shows a few key examples.

Figure 2.3
Purpose and Matching Priorities

Space/Category	What Is the Purpose?	Priorities That Match the Purpose
Teacher work-space	• Place for teacher to complete work • House teacher materials	• Have a functional desk or table space to store laptop and stationery, plan, and collaborate
Bulletin boards	• Display authentic student work • Show student learning • Student use and reference points	• Showcase processes of student learning • Post student-generated and coconstructed anchors
Furniture	• Provide comfortable and varied seating arrangements for students	• Meet student comfort and safety needs
Central consumable materials storage	• Classroom community use	• Students can be curious and creative with materials • Students have easy access to sharpened pencils, coloring tools, scissors, glue, and other common materials used in learning activities
Center areas for math, literacy, reading corner mat or rug area	• Student engagement • Student access to materials to support learning • Space to encourage frequent reading or game playing to enhance literacy or math skills	• Meet student learning needs • Create an area for collaborative work

Lists will undoubtedly be a bit different depending on the context in which you work or depending on the condition in which you moved into the space. Your spaces may be different, but the purpose may not. Additionally, the same area may have different priorities depending on your school, your cohort, or your age group. However, by completing this process, you may likely find that physically listing out your spaces and the resources in them will help you realize how much "stuff" is packed into the room.

Step 4

So far, we have tackled the purpose and priority elements of the framework. So what is left for us to address? That's right: pare it down, which could be one of the more challenging of the Triple P framework. It is now time to take the work we have completed in identifying the real purpose and priorities, and use it to help us proceed to this final, crucial element of the framework in Figure 2.4.

Once you have completed your list, you should have an unobstructed view of what items are not supporting the primary purpose or priority of that space. If you keep items stored in that space and they do not serve your intended purpose, nor do they match your priorities, it is time to find a new home for them. In fact, most teachers can remove 10–15 items from the classroom and still be fully functional, as author Bob Dillon stated in a *Cult of Pedagogy* guest blog feature called "12 Ways to Upgrade Your Classroom Design" (Gonzalez, 2018).

Figure 2.4
Paring Down Your Resources

Area	How Can I Pare This Down?
Teacher work-space	• Keep out only the items used on a daily basis, such as a planner, one pad of sticky notes, a pen, a pencil, and a marker. • In the desk drawers or other storage areas, keep items limited to what would be consumed within one month. • Other items that are seldomly used can be stored in the closet or can find a new home for someone else to use (outlined later in Provocations).
Bulletin boards	• Remove outdated postings. • Post only items that enhance learning for reference and reflection on main boards.
Furniture	• Remove broken furniture or fix it quickly. • Use existing furniture and space creatively to maximize space use, such as turning a shelf on its side to use as a workspace on one side and storage on the other.

continued

Figure 2.4 *(continued)*
Paring Down Your Resources

Area	How Can I Pare This Down?
Central consumable materials storage	• Keep consumables in a central location for community use. • Keep only essentials for the number of students and replenish only when necessary. • Keep extra supplies in the class closet.
Center areas for math, literacy, reading corner mat or rug area	• Keep mostly unit-related items out so you can cycle items for student use without overcrowding space.

Provocations to Sustain Your Decluttered Environment

Now that you are ready to clear out the clutter and make room for a more purposeful and intentional working space, where will all the remaining items go? We may be striving to have a clutter-free space to learn in, but we do not want to needlessly add to overflowing landfill spaces. Below we have compiled a few tips that you may want to consider when decluttering your physical environment.

1. Making Decisions with a Mystery Box

Bestselling author Gretchen Rubin has come up with an idea to help you deal with those miscellaneous items that you feel like you might need but get put away and not touched again. In her blog post "A Yearly Challenge" (2019b), Rubin suggests putting your miscellaneous items into a mystery box. These items may not have a home, you may not be sure what to do with them, nor are you convinced they will be necessary. She suggests dating the box when you put it together, and if a year has gone by and you have not needed anything in that box, then it is time to discard it. In this way, you have given these miscellaneous items a home in case they are needed, and you have also given yourself an easy way to decide what will happen to them in the end. You could also create other similar habits or routines to help you make decisions about what is truly needed to meet your purpose in your physical environment.

2. Have a Pick-up Event

Take photos of the items and send an e-mail to see if other teachers need things. Give a deadline for response and pick-up. If you have items left over, ask your administrator about how to store the leftovers or if there is a charity or nonprofit organization that accepts supplies and will pick up the items from the school. If you have old workbooks or textbooks, consider locating nonprofit organizations, rehabilitation centers, or other learning centers. If you have old furniture that you would like removed, arrange for the proper personnel to pick it up and remove it for you (or perhaps you can find another purpose for it in your classroom or elsewhere).

3. Create a Giving Table

On WeAreTeachers.com, Natali Petricic (2018) suggests another alternative to creating a shared space: a giving table, or space in which teachers can place items they no longer need that may be enriching in other teacher's classrooms. By creating this giving space, we are not throwing away and wasting materials but instead finding an alternative home where they will be wanted and used. Continue to consider, though, that we would not want this giving table to morph into a trash table, with unwanted items sitting idle for months at a time. If something has been left unwanted for a set time, it may be that the item is no longer usable at all and needs to be discarded thoughtfully in a permanent fashion.

4. Shared Resource Spaces

One option that may work for your school context is to create a shared resources space somewhere within the school. Organizing and having this space available will assist you in minimizing the clutter in your physical area, reduce the possibility of discarding items wanted by others, and help in avoiding duplicate resources (i.e., physical and economic waste) within your school.

This can take the form of a resource library, where each staff member can check out what they need for however long they need it. A room such as this can run particularly efficiently if it houses resources required for a unit of work that may only come up for two weeks a year. However, be mindful of how this space is used and maintained. The last thing we need is to create a dumping ground in which no one wants to enter in fear of never getting back out again!

5. Trial Removals

Not ready to commit to permanent removal of your stuff? As mentioned above, Dillon has told us that in all likelihood, we can remove 10–15 items and keep the functionality of the space intact. But what if this feels like an overcommitment right now? Perhaps think about giving yourself a trial removal period instead. The key is to "subtract" items from the space, and you can do this on a trial basis to really help you see whether you needed those subtracted items or not. Set the trial within a certain timeline, or give yourself a trial deadline, to avoid creating a new set of clutter. After time has passed, you will be able to make clearer judgments about whether the items are needed or not.

Final Considerations When Decluttering the Physical Space

Thoughtfulness for Colleagues

A note here about decluttering items that may belong, be owned, or used by others around the school: While you may be very keen to throw yourself wholeheartedly into clearing away everything you feel is unnecessary, removing items that are used by others is a clear path to create friction between you and your colleagues. Be very mindful about things that others may feel are still valuable or necessary, and find an agreed-upon system for moving and housing said items that are acceptable to all parties.

In a similar vein, be wary of expecting others to express thanks or appreciation for your efforts in decluttering. Do not wait for others' cooperation or buy-in before feeling like you can start the process. If you decide to embark on the process of decluttering your physical environment, you need to do it for yourself. For those around you, it may not fit within their purpose or priorities right now. As we know, nagging or pushing people, or consistently telling them they are wrong to not join in the decluttering efforts, will not lead to positive interactions. Do what you need to in order to create a purposeful and welcoming space while still being respectful of your colleagues.

Stop the Tide

You have now spent valuable time decluttering your physical spaces to refocus them on the purpose and priorities they were designed for. Budgeting time comes around and you can't help wondering if you will be replacing your old clutter with new items instead! Not only is this a waste of resources, but you will also be setting yourself up for a second round of decluttering in the future. So when completing your order for the next school year, consider the following aspects:

- How will this item help meet my purpose in the teaching and learning context?
- How will this item help meet my priorities in the teaching and learning context?
- Do I already have an item similar to this that I can use instead?
- Would I be able to borrow a similar item from someone else instead of buying a duplicate?
- How much use will I get out of this item over the course of the school year?

To sustain your newly established minimalist environment, you will need to be the filter for all new items coming into your room. Unfortunately, the build-up of new clutter will not just be a result of school budget purchases. Additionally, if you return to your saving-every-possible-item ways, your clutter will also return. Be intentional in making choices and actions in this area! You have invested a lot of time and energy into creating a new space, so adopt this new habit and be consistent.

Avoid the Organization Trap

It can feel satisfying to get your physical environment tidy, decluttered, and organized. However, sometimes we fall into the trap of wasting time and money in the process of organizing without actually serving our real purpose of why we are doing it in the first place. Ever felt like you just could not get started on that project without a new notebook and some new pens? Have you experienced feeling like you couldn't start writing your reports without alphabetizing and color-coding your assessment file? Have you ever spent time creating colored and laminated signs before you could get down to your actual planning or grading? This "reorganizing" is procrastinating. Also, you have just added more clutter in your environment! If we have effectively decluttered using the Triple P Framework, perhaps these boxes, files, and labels may not even be necessary. We know—stationery stores are the best. But if we are striving to meet our true purpose, perhaps our biggest priority should not be on getting everything "organized" before we start our real work.

Confronting Emotional Resistance to Decluttering Your Classroom

Many experts have written about the emotional connection people have to things and the difficulties that people may have in getting rid of items. Every iteration of the TV show *Hoarders* is about just that. This emotional reaction may well enter into the physical spaces of our classrooms, too. We are sure to have known a teacher or two in our time who could not let anything go, in case it could be useful somehow or sometime in the future. If you find yourself having these kinds of strong emotions and reactions, despite having the intention and wish to declutter, here are some resources for you to explore:

- The International OCD Foundation has information and links to resources about hoarding (www.hoarding.iocdf.org).
- A simple search on the American Psychiatric Association will lead you to many articles, FAQs, and stories about hoarding (www.psychiatry.org).
- The Peace of Mind Foundation also features helpful resources, including online avenues of support (www.peaceofmind.com).

In Conclusion

Chapter Takeaways

- Getting rid of everything is not necessary!
- Be aware that a scarcity mindset may be encouraging you to hold on to unnecessary resources.
- Use the Triple P framework to help you consider each element of your classroom space.
- Be careful when decluttering items that may be used by others.
- Consider creating spaces for shared resources, or a giving table for passing on items to those who may need them more.
- Avoid using your budget to reclutter your room!

- Don't waste time or money on unnecessary organization.
- Assistance is available if you recognize any discomfort or emotional resistance to decluttering.

Lingering Question

How do I get others on board with this process so I do not feel alone?

Up Next

In Chapter 3, we take you through an in-depth assessment of the initiatives used at your school. This chapter is a big one to tackle and can be viewed as though it is an administrator's responsibility to declutter initiatives; however, many schools value the voice of teachers when choosing new initiatives or when evaluating current ones. We will use the Triple P process and thinking frameworks to help you weed through the initiative clutter. So let's go!

3

Decluttering Initiatives

The Problem: Initiative Clutter

Does the thought of making sense of all our school-based initiatives make you feel a bit dismal? Well, you can let yourself sink into an abyss, or you can look at the bigger picture of why you feel this way and dig into how to remedy the feelings about the clutter associated with educational initiatives.

Could we make an assumption and say that it is a common experience for teachers (and schools in general) in every pocket of the world to be flooded with initiative options? Because of the challenges inherent in education, there is an overabundance of initiatives and programs presented to rescue us and help us solve these problems of practice. Is the challenge low reading levels? There are several initiatives your school can buy into to solve that. Are the teachers struggling to teach science because they do not have the content knowledge or do not have enough items to do experiments with? Never fear! All teachers will go to the same training and get new science kits. Behavior problems? Done! There are tons of initiatives to help you regulate behaviors using a range of motivators and rewards.

In their book *Creative Schools: The Grassroots Revolution That's Transforming Education* (2015), coauthors Sir Ken Robinson and Lou Aronica state that "modern education systems are cluttered with every sort of distraction. There are political agendas, national priorities, union bargaining positions, building codes" (p. 71). These initiatives might be offered as systemic transitions to new standards. They may be newly packaged curricula to be adopted at the school or regional level as a result of a nationwide transition. We may be looking at a set of educational jargon based around the next trend in education on a global scale, or a new communication plan to test with families.

These experiences might be called initiatives, but really they are recycled ideas, approaches, or strategies that have been floating around in education for decades and given a catchy new name, leading to a career-long dose of initiative fatigue. Fellow ASCD author and Emeritus Head of New City Schools in St. Louis, Missouri, Thomas Hoerr told us, "Simply adding programs—even if they're good programs—leads to faculty frustration and inefficiency. Instead, we should step back and analyze our mission statement: What is our school supposed to do and why is it important? From there, we should prioritize, cut, prioritize again, and focus on a few important initiatives." First, we pare this down to what an initiative actually is: a new idea to improve something that needs it or to do something independently. Independent initiatives may be more visible in your school, yet big initiatives generally come from the top down.

What Decluttering Initiatives Means and Why It Is Important

Decluttering initiatives means wading through and making good choices about the myriad of theories, programs, and approaches to education that are available to us. While these initiatives may have been proposed by the administrative team, the superintendent at the district office, or a state or national government agency, it is the responsibility of administrators and their teacher teams to sift through a required initiative or program to find the most salient, effective elements. This also means that while some initiatives are mandates, others are not. This chapter will help teachers evaluate and prioritize what they must do about initiatives and identify what extraneous initiative "clutter" can be cut.

For the purpose of our book, we will be examining and siphoning through initiatives using the Triple P framework. Let's funnel this idea and examine the reasons why one would declutter initiatives through the lens of a class-room teacher or school-based coach. It may seem obvious to just have less initiatives given to us, right? However, the reality of introducing initiatives can be anything but simple.

Meghan Everette, a mathematics coach for Salt Lake City School District, remembers the initiative fatigue of when she was a full-time classroom teacher. She tries to best reduce that stress with the teachers she coaches by presenting the essential elements of a program first (the prioritizing part of the Triple P), so as not to unleash everything on teachers at once. The challenge then becomes knowing when to release additional pieces of the puzzle to teachers. At some point, other elements of the new initiative will need to be addressed. But knowing when, in what order, and how to time this out will be necessary in a coach's planning. It's a delicate system of strategic decision making by the coach and the teachers. We want to avoid situations where we put the cart before the horse, need to apply the brakes, and then wonder why the cart irretrievably rolled down the hill.

Now, let's look at the what and the why through a teacher's lens. On the ASCD Whole Child Blog, classroom teacher Kevin Parr wrote a post titled "Keep Students and Parents (and Teachers) Initiative Fatigue Free" (2014), addressing this need for less within his own experience. In the post he mentions that he was always wondering about all the things he wasn't doing, stating that "[t]here was too much, too fast, and with too little time for me to evaluate or prioritize the ideas coming at me, let alone do anything with them. I was overwhelmed and anxious. I was lost." Unfortunately, Kevin is not alone in feeling this way.

Examples like this make us realize that approaching teaching with a minimalist lens is not easy. We get that overwhelming sensation even when thinking about all the items on our to-read, to-make, to-learn lists. Our time is valuable, and initiatives can be time intensive to learn and implement. Some initiatives may be expensive to purchase and might not at all be what you need to support you and your students in the classroom. When a chunk of time and a substantial amount of effort are required to learn something that may or may not be valuable in practice, this can be deemed as time and intellectual waste. Teachers like Kevin often state that there is never enough time in a day, week, or school year to cover all the standards, content, and other material. Above and beyond this, we are still left wondering about what else we should be doing!

Thus, when confronted with an initiative that does not directly coincide with your school's mission, vision, program, or population, we can anticipate levels of animosity. Because time is a precious commodity, it is essential to be able to find purpose, prioritize, and pare down all the clutter. In her blog article "Work-Life Balance: Saying No Can Make You a Better Teacher," Sarah Knutson (2018) highlights the need to plan with intention in the time-frame set aside specifically for planning. This planning can include weeding through initiatives and decluttering the mental space needed to find the valuable pieces to bring forward for students. There will always be some initiatives that become mandates, this is a given, so it is essential to think big picture and strip away the unnecessary pieces and trim those initiatives so they work within your existing realm.

Now, is it strange of us to bring forth this minimalist initiative to you? Not at all, because you came to us. You see the value in transforming your current teaching approach to one that can release the burden of initiative fatigue. You are not only transforming your teaching life through minimalism, you are approaching life with a new lens and approach. And that has the potential to significantly change your teaching experience.

The Cycle Elements for Initiatives

Act. This chapter is a continuation of the Act phase of the cycle. This *paring down* process will take a good chunk of your time and energy because it focuses on two sets of initiative decision making: whether to adopt an initiative and then what to do when you have adopted it.

*Note: You will likely find yourself continuing to work in the Inquire and Investigate phases of your Triple P cycle here, too.

Triple P Decision Making for Initial Initiative Adoption

The sense of urgency to solve problems quickly pushes us into this thinking that a problem is easily solved and that a program can be the answer. In reality, if we pare down our thinking about the challenges at hand, it could be possible to address them by thinking more intentionally and by making use of our existing resources.

We have had a chance to discuss various elements related to the decisions needed when decluttering initiatives, and we provided some examples about how this may play out in real-life contexts. But first, you and your team will need to determine whether the initiative will actually be adopted. In Figure 3.1, we have arranged these main ideas into a decision-making flowchart to aid you in onboarding new initiatives. To ease the mental congestion of overwhelming choices, we can ask ourselves some initial Triple P questions.

Triple P Funneling

Now that a decision has been made to adopt an initiative, you will need to work through your initiative funneling and questioning, like in Figure 3.2, to find the pieces of the initiative that support the reason you made the decision to implement this initiative in your classroom or school.

As we introduced earlier, we are in a constant state of swimming through seaweed when faced with educational initiatives. The first step is to recognize the overwhelming amount of stuff to go through. After you know the decisions you face, you can move forward to focus on identifying your purpose in the options you have. We have provided a list of example initiative purposes in Appendix B if you are challenged with identifying your purpose with clarity.

Using Triple P with Familiar Initiatives

New program names and new sets of jargon can make teachers cringe. And while we would like to believe these initiatives are designed as a support to your practice and help practitioners work through challenges, schools can purchase them with rosy aspirations that they'll solve every problem, as we have mentioned above. Either can be true depending on your experience in finding purpose, capability to adapt and prioritize, and know-how to pare down effectively.

Figure 3.1
Initial Triple P Decision-Making Flowchart for Initiative Adoption

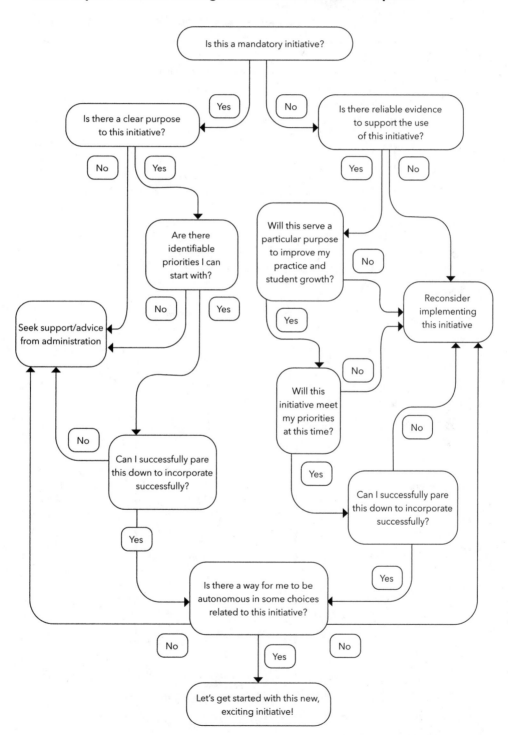

Figure 3.2

Initiative Triple P Questions and Decision Making

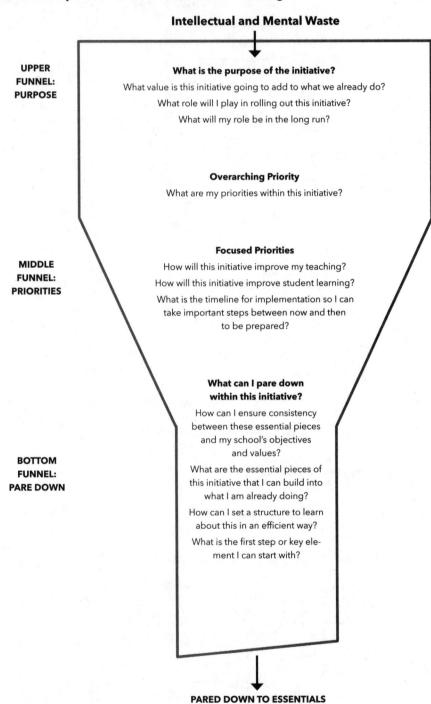

Intellectual and Mental Waste

UPPER FUNNEL: PURPOSE

What is the purpose of the initiative?
What value is this initiative going to add to what we already do?
What role will I play in rolling out this initiative?
What will my role be in the long run?

Overarching Priority
What are my priorities within this initiative?

MIDDLE FUNNEL: PRIORITIES

Focused Priorities
How will this initiative improve my teaching?
How will this initiative improve student learning?
What is the timeline for implementation so I can take important steps between now and then to be prepared?

BOTTOM FUNNEL: PARE DOWN

What can I pare down within this initiative?
How can I ensure consistency between these essential pieces and my school's objectives and values?
What are the essential pieces of this initiative that I can build into what I am already doing?
How can I set a structure to learn about this in an efficient way?
What is the first step or key element I can start with?

PARED DOWN TO ESSENTIALS

Let's look at a couple of examples here. Do you remember the reading wars? These were the competing ideas that children learn to read by decoding or by using a whole-language approach (Strauss, 2018). This long-standing debate resulted in educators everywhere experiencing this familiar conundrum. We swung from new programs for decoding to ones for a whole-language approach. Eventually, and perhaps better yet, balanced literacy was born, and thus, a very popular program included both sets of ideologies in one synthesized program created by Fountas and Pinnell.

We can connect that now to articles and blogs about balance in life, generally. Have you read about balance in life from multiple sources over the years? That balance can be one key element to success when faced with new initiatives, so let's apply this philosophy in Figure 3.3.

Ask yourself: what is new and solution-oriented about balanced literacy? When you pare it down, balanced literacy is a combination of decoding and whole-language approaches, which are not new ideas. Perhaps it is the amalgamation of those two ideas, in conjunction with teacher creativity and autonomous decision making within implementation, that is innovative. Weaving this all together and synthesizing it with your knowledge of student strengths and areas of development will be demonstrated in student reading success. This process of sorting out your purpose, knowing your priorities for the program, and knowing how to pare down can make decluttering, a once-massive undertaking, into something very manageable.

A second example of initiative adoption might be related to social-emotional learning. Like minimalism, social-emotional learning is an approach that is also an enormous umbrella under which streams of intertwining related concepts are interconnected, such as trauma, self-esteem, emotions, and acceptance. It is a web of connected ideas, each of which can come along with its own toolkit. We can then look forward to a new set of cards, a new word wheel, or a guide for you to purchase and use. These tools can all be very helpful, but they can also push you into a resource oblivion. Previously we have discussed the research and the "research" behind initiatives. There is certainly plenty of solid background for the necessity to emotionally support students and spend time developing relationships with them. From this, teachers can then make choices about how this will be embedded in everyday school life. For them, this process of sorting out the purpose, knowing their priorities for the program, and identifying their "already-knowns" for paring down has been supported already by reliable research.

Provocations to Sustain Your Decluttered Initiatives

We have examined scenarios in which we might feel overwhelmed because of available choices, but we also discussed feeling comfort in returning to the known. These powerful emotions are commonplace, and we have all experienced them in some way within our own contexts. From this point, we will

Figure 3.3

A Comparison Chart of Familiar or Potential Initiatives Using Triple P

Balanced Literacy		
Upper Funnel Triple P Questions	Middle Funnel Triple P	Pared-Down Thinking
What is the purpose of balanced literacy for us?	• Why would I bring balanced literacy into my classroom? • What will I learn from this approach? • What are the essential pieces of balanced literacy? • How does this build on the positives that are already happening within my context? • What role will I play in the rolling out of this initiative?	• Balanced literacy is a well-rounded program that combines two important parts for student reading development: the use of decoding and whole language. • I might learn new research behind how students learn to read and some practical strategies to support my existing readers.
What are our priorities within balanced literacy?	• What is the most important part of balanced literacy for my students? • Will learning about and using aspects of balanced literacy improve my teaching? • Will this initiative improve student learning? • Has this been mandated? If so, is there room to move something else off the plate to make time? • What is the timeline for implementation so I can take steps between now and then to be prepared?	• The essential parts of balanced literacy include modeled, guided, shared, and independent literary components. • I already do three of these.

Balanced Literacy		
Upper Funnel Triple P Questions	Middle Funnel Triple P	Pared-Down Thinking
What can we pare down within the balanced literacy approach?	• How will I learn about this in an efficient way and not feel overwhelmed? • What is the first step or key element that I can start with? • What aspects of balanced literacy am I already doing, or are similar to what I am already doing?	• I can likely build the last element into other areas such as social studies and science to ensure literacy components are evident in all parts of the day. • I could build in choice to ensure students have some autonomy in literacy so they can model for and guide each other, too. • I can invite the literacy coach in to co-teach and support another group of students.
Social-Emotional Learning		
What is the purpose of our SEL initiative?	• What are the specific reasons for integrating SEL? • How will the school benefit as a whole? • How will individuals benefit? How will specific groups benefit?	• We know that learning about each student and their emotional needs will positively affect their learning. • We can tell that students need support in expressing their feelings.
What are our priorities within our SEL initiative?	• What pieces need to be learned first? • What parts will we rollout first, and why? • What is the timeline? • How can we do this holistically?	• We can anticipate some positive relationship development between students as well as with teachers. • Students may feel comfortable and safe to share. • This may also improve home life as students transfer strategies for home.
What can we pare down within the SEL initiative?	• Are there other resources we need, or can we use our existing resources? Who and how? • How can we build this into what we are already doing?	• We already have counselors to support students, but we can build in some emotional literacy and vocabulary building practices into existing classes. • We could use simple emotion wheels. • We can build in some optional meditations or calming practices to help alleviate any stressors in the day.

continued

Figure 3.3 (*continued*)

A Comparison Chart of Familiar or Potential Initiatives Using Triple P

STEM or STEAM		
Upper Funnel Triple P Questions	Middle Funnel Triple P	Pared-Down Thinking
What is the purpose of STEAM in our school?	• Why would we bring STEAM into our school? • What will we learn from this approach? • What are the essential pieces of implementing STEAM to ensure its quality? • How does this build on the positives that are already happening within my context? • What role will I play in rolling out this initiative?	• Our district has been awarded funds to incorporate STEAM education. • We all have to learn about STEAM education. • We already have great arts and science programs, so perhaps we can build out from our existing programming.
What are our priorities within our STEAM initiative?	• What is the most important part of STEAM for my students? • Will learning about and using aspects of STEAM improve my teaching? • Will this initiative improve student learning? • Has this been mandated? If so, is there room to move something else off the plate to make time? • What is the timeline for implementation so I can take important steps between now and then to be prepared? • How will we collaborate to meet the requirements of STEAM?	• I will need to meet with science and arts teachers to discuss building more engineering into our learning experiences. • We will need to make sure we have collaborative meeting times.

STEM or STEAM		
What can we pare down within STEM/ STEAM to suit us?	• Are there other resources we need, or can we use our existing resources? Who and how? • How can we build this into what we are already doing?	• We can plan to look at existing kits, tools, and physical hands-on pieces for student consumption and creation and use what we already have, rather than purchasing more in initial stages. • If we have to give purchase options to the administration team, we will plan to use money for student hands-on experiences, consumables, and staff to support quality learning. • We have many parents who work in the sciences/engineering/arts who we can tap as guest speakers and workshop leaders for innovation approaches to implementing this initiative.

begin identifying our own places in this process to find purpose, prioritize, and pare down initiatives to help ignite teacher capacity.

Rogers's Diffusion of Innovation

When decluttering educational initiatives, it can be critical to engage in self-reflection about what a change will mean for you and your practice. Rogers's (2003) model in *Diffusion of Innovations* points out many important factors when a new initiative is introduced to a group. People will generally go through a predictable set of steps when taking on board a new program or idea. Rogers's five steps in adopting a new initiative are knowledge, persuasion, decision, implementation, and confirmation. When you feel overwhelmed by a new initiative, remember these stages and know that we all need time to build knowledge, be persuaded, and have a go when trying something new, as seen in Figure 3.4.

Figure 3.4

Rogers's Adoption Stages Aligned to the Cycle

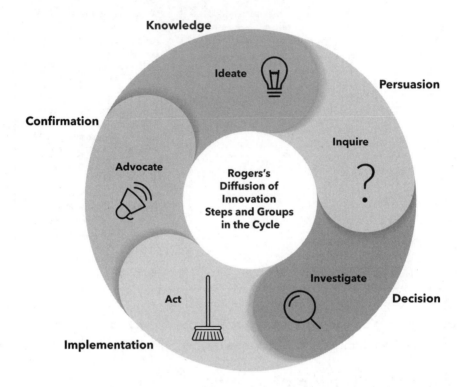

In addition to all of us progressing similarly through these stages, Rogers discusses how in every group of people, there will be different levels of enthusiasm for jumping on board with new ideas. At the forefront of any group are the innovators (2.5%) and early adopters (13.5%), who will be ready to try something new and get excited for new applications to their world. Following those groups are the early and late majorities (34% and 34%) and, finally, the laggards (16%), who will resist change at all costs. We've taken these groups and loosely placed them alongside our cycle for a comparative. In Figure 3.5, we have further defined these groups and offer some specific suggestions to find purpose and priorities within initiatives and then pare down the essentials and details.

As you read through Rogers's innovation groups, reflect on where you typically fall when a new change comes around within your context. Know that you're not alone in your perspective and that you will pass through the same stages as everyone else, and hopefully you can move from feeling overwhelmed with the multitude of choices to feeling comfortable and confident in your decluttering initiatives.

Let's now take a closer look into these three groups: the innovators and early adopters, the majority, and the laggards. Depending on where you see yourself within these groups, your approach to find the purpose, priorities, and subsequently pare down changes in your context will likely look a little different. So in addition to the work already outlined, we want to consider some strategies that will be directly related to where each group should go next.

Figure 3.5
Rogers's Diffusion of Innovation Groups

For the innovators and early adopters:

Be reflective about yourself, and understand that your eagerness to have a go also means that you are willing to take the risk of failure. While we love this about you, be cognizant of wasting too much of your precious time on ineffective practices! Additionally, the majority will be looking to you to take cues on which new initiatives to incorporate into their practice. Be responsible about what you encourage others to do. When considering the purpose of a new initiative, think carefully about whether this is really going to be something innovative that is necessary to your practice. Will this bring about effective transformation, or does this look the same as something you are already doing? You will need to take time to think about your priorities and whether you can feasibly take another initiative on (we know you are already trying out a whole smorgasbord of new projects as it is!) and do this new program, and your students, justice.

For the majority:

This entire chapter is for you! We know the majority of teachers like to see some proof that new initiatives are effective or necessary. Our hope is that the ideas and suggestions made throughout this chapter are useful to you as you consider what to take on board and in what capacity. Use the Triple P questions and funnel to help inform your decisions and move forward in decluttering initiatives.

For those who need to idle a little longer on change:

We recognize that these initiatives may feel like the same ideas being recycled in new packaging with some new catchy acronym to go along with it! We would encourage you to really take the time to think about the school's purpose in bringing this to you.

Have recent schoolwide results been less than pleasing, and is the school legitimately trying to improve student learning? Has this been mandated, and is the school doing everything it can to operate legally and maintain its accreditation?

How does this align with the school's priorities? Has this initiative been brought about to address the school's improvement plan? Maybe the area that needs paring down is our resistance to change and our wish to continue the way we have always been. And by all means, wait to see how things have gone for the innovators and early adopters! Learn from their mistakes, and join in the adventure to ensure you are purposeful in your practice.

Building Your Capacity

Thoonen, Sleegers, Oort, Peetsma, and Geijsel (2011) found that your confidence in new initiatives and organizational goals is directly related to the extent to which you have a say in the decision-making process. Therefore, being involved in the decisions when adopting new initiatives results in feeling more committed to the change. This is a fundamental element of developing teacher capacity, and it does not lie in the hands of your administrator. It is up to you to build your own capacity and seek support along the way.

Teachers should be encouraged to take on new initiatives to achieve the best possible growth and performance for themselves, their students, and the wider school community. Is this a model you currently use or envision yourself participating in? Teachers at Brandon Johnson's (2019) school in Fort Worth, Texas, live this experience. Johnson, as principal and disruptive educator, provides support for teachers developing their own leadership capacities. Not only does he ensure there is teacher voice in initiative adoption, but he also guides teachers through initiative development and implementation processes that they have a passion for.

The idea of building your own capacity as a teacher doesn't have to be a solitary event, but as shown in Figure 3.6, you must acknowledge the role that motivation and self-esteem have in work performance. It is also crucial to consider institutional knowledge and teacher leadership and who may leave for a new position in a year's time. And above all, building your capacity as a teacher results in improved educational experiences for students.

In fact, Thoonen et al. (2011) found that self-efficacy and motivation were primary factors in both teacher learning and teaching practices. Some of the strategies that support your capacity as a teacher also allow you and your colleagues to take on roles of leadership, participate in school leadership team meetings, and share teacher expertise. On the other hand, when our ability to participate in decision making is minimal, our effectiveness is limited and our commitment toward organizational goals can become close to nonexistent.

This is similarly reflected in students' development of agency. When we empower students to take ownership of their learning, they are more engaged and enthusiastic. When we limit their agency, their education is passive. This, too, happens in teachers when our choices are limited or denied. When we talk about decluttering initiatives, we need to find a way to feel like we have some ownership in what we take on so that we do not feel detached from the process and rattled by the clutter of forced new approaches and tasks. Through active involvement in the decision making, we will increase our motivation for new initiatives and subsequently improve efficacy in our work with students and the school.

Figure 3.6
Building Capacity

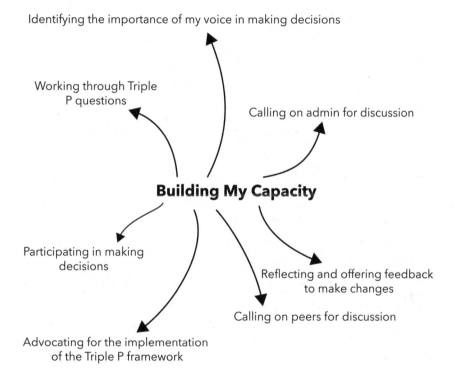

Identifying the importance of my voice in making decisions

Working through Triple P questions

Calling on admin for discussion

Building My Capacity

Participating in making decisions

Reflecting and offering feedback to make changes

Calling on peers for discussion

Advocating for the implementation of the Triple P framework

Pushing Back

By now a clearer picture should be starting to emerge about how to see our way through our roles in decluttering initiatives. We have discussed why onboarding initiatives can become so overwhelming, and we have introduced some concepts that can help us develop more comfort and confidence to make good choices for ourselves as educators.

But what if we do not have any choice? What if we do not have the good fortune to find a context in which our leaders have recognized the importance of developing teacher agency and choice? School contexts do have the potential to feel like we are getting swept along with a runaway train. So how do we effectively push back on initiatives that are mandated when we feel we cannot get on board? In this case, we would encourage everyone to approach this issue in the most professional way possible, even when it feels impossible. Turning away from change, refusing to participate, sending urgent e-mails to all staff, or publicly denouncing the initiative at every possible opportunity will probably not get us very far! Here are some suggestions to respectfully push back while building your capacity to be heard:

1. Take a step back from the situation to reflect and let any strong emotional reactions diffuse.

2. Talk to your trusted colleagues for their views and input.

3. Plan out and frame a discussion around the Triple P questions to keep the dialogue focused.

4. Seek out an administrator you can have further discussions with.

5. Approach your discussion with growth, development, and collegiality. And above all, be respectful and be careful about expectations to get everything you want from the first conversation!

6. Find out as much as you can about what the purpose and priorities are around this new initiative and offer solutions, such as being on a team to pare down the initiative.

7. Return to your administrator with feedback about the process and the value it adds to clarity of purpose and focus on priorities.

Gemma Cass, teacher and lecturer in primary education in the UK, encourages us to take listening as our first action. She points out that we all have the right to question what is happening, but it is important to try to understand the culture and values of the school as well as the position of our school leaders before rushing to judgment. She says, "Try and listen with an open mind first, before making a judgment." She goes on to encourage us to find a balance between being our authentic selves and taking a neutral, professional stance.

We have worked through a lot of decluttering in this chapter, and now it's time for you to identify your next action. Remember you can use Appendix B to help focus your attention on pinpointing your purpose and priorities. Once that piece is clarified, you can choose a provocation to pare down your initiatives.

In Conclusion

Chapter Takeaways

- Initiatives can be chosen based on how they supplement already effective systems.
- Initiatives can be molded to fit contexts.
- Building your capacity as a teacher can support the effectiveness of new initiatives.
- Stay true to your values and beliefs when adopting initiatives.

Lingering Question

What can I do to have more say in how new initiatives are adopted?

Up Next

In the next chapter, there may be some answers to the lingering question above. In Chapter 4, we tackle an enormous piece of your work as a teacher: your curriculum. You can expect to learn about some of the problems we face when we have so many curriculum materials. We'll walk through the Triple P framework to get organized without losing integrity in what you are using to teach your students.

Decluttering the Curriculum

The Problem: Overloaded Content and Planning Resources

Curriculum is an essential element of education and one we generally refer to as the "what" of teaching. These are the skills and understandings we want our students to have by the time they leave us. Usually arranged by grade or age band, these skills and understandings are paced out across the course of students' careers at school. For our purposes, we are going to consider the curriculum as two separate pieces. The first what of the curriculum is the standards or benchmarks your school must use as the content for learning. The second what is the planning resources we use to help us deliver or teach these standards. This could be the units of study you write or the textbooks or programs your school uses. We want to delineate between these two, as in all probability, you will have much more control over one than the other in your work as a teacher. Unless you work in a dedicated curriculum department or role, teachers have little say in what standards they are expected to teach. In order to feel effective and productive, you should focus your energy on areas where you have control. So, our emphasis in this chapter will focus on the elements that you can influence within your context.

The Cycle Element for Curriculum Decluttering

Act. Here you will continue the action of decluttering, focusing not only on how to pare down physical curriculum resources but also on decluttering mental waste.

*Note: You may find yourself doing some additional inquiring and investigating into some of the research and other elements of the decluttering process for your curriculum.

Types of Curriculum

Generally, schools have a couple of options when it comes to the curriculum. In many schools around the world, the curriculum is chosen for teachers, and they teach it with fidelity. In some schools, teachers have some leeway to use the chosen curriculum as the primary source for content, or they can use it as a supplement within a partially teacher-created curriculum. In other schools, the curriculum is created by teachers, and they are free to use a number of resources both provided by the school and chosen autonomously by teachers to create a unique program for students. Whichever type of curriculum you implement, segmented out in Figure 4.1, focusing your time and devoting your energy to the essentials of your curriculum, the pieces that matter most, will make a world of difference.

The Twin Sins of Planning

In *Upgrade Your Teaching*, McTighe and Willis (2019) talk about what they describe as the "twin sins of planning." The first sin they discuss is the trap some teachers fall into when they focus on activity-oriented planning, when teachers get caught in fun or cute activities that may not necessarily result

Figure 4.1
Curriculum Flowchart

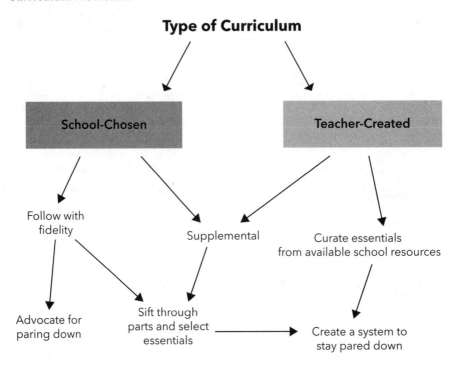

in deep or lasting student understanding. The second sin McTighe and Willis discuss is the preoccupation with coverage, to simply cover the required content and graze across the standards. The authors discuss these aspects of curriculum to highlight ways in which teachers get distracted or tangled in their planning and thus move away from our purpose and priorities to ensure education is meaningful and long-lasting.

When considering the first sin of activity-oriented planning, we must think about the prevalence of social media and the continuously evolving face of Pinterest-worthy classroom setups or eye-catching activities on Instagram. This creates an awareness of what teachers are doing in their classrooms all over the world, at any given moment. These sites can no doubt spark inspiration, but they can also serve as a distraction from our true purpose of teaching and learning effectively. The internet is tangled with sites crowded with photo posts of activities that look like an appealing and engaging way to address a skill or concept. Many of these activities only offer a few minutes of eye-sparkle for ambivalent students, and then they are ignored for the rest of the year.

Sadly, this is not a sustainable way to curate your curriculum resources. Here we would consider the types of waste we mentioned earlier in the book when we consider the amount of teacher money, time to prepare, and the burden of comparison that teachers can entrench themselves in emotionally because they feel that they do not measure up. While we hope that the time spent searching would lead to potentially increased opportunity for engaging professional learning and the ready ability to learn from thought leaders, it can also lead us into more damaging trends such as unnecessarily high levels of time and energy waste. The time spent looking at things that will not add value to our curriculum bank may in actuality cause us to waste our greatest asset: our motivation and drive to be a skilled educator.

Please know that we do not wish to dismiss the hours of time and effort that teachers use to create things that may be interesting to their students, or negate the intention behind teachers' creative efforts. We are asking you to proceed with caution. Be thoughtful with your time. We want to nudge you into entering unknown territory, get a little uncomfortable and spend your time decluttering so you do not get lost in "stuff" that you are used to getting lost in. We want you to stop losing your most important resource and extrapolate what you need in order to be the best teacher you can be for your students. Once you have worked through the framework, then you can sprinkle in some jazzy bits of Pinterest and Instagram later. Eventually, though, you may find that once you have worked through this process, you will veer away from the shiny objects and plan more for depth rather than breadth, and that will keep your prep time to a minimum. Know that this process will mean spending time up front curating your existing curriculum and associated resources in order to find the most direct route possible to meet the needs of your students.

When considering McTighe and Willis's (2019) second sin to overfocus on coverage, let us consider that there seems to be a belief that teachers need help on more *what* to teach. So publishing companies create ample amounts of predetermined packaged programs for schools to purchase and for teachers to implement in their classrooms (these often also address the "how," which will be further evaluated in Chapter 5). Publishers promote their latest and greatest update to ensure teachers know that their product is standards-aligned and research-based, that it is high-interest *and* leveled! All of this sounds fantastic and can allow for a potentially easy decision to make. But this does not necessarily result in making teaching easier or better. These teaching resources do have a place in particular classes, in certain contexts, in varying regions of the world. But it needs to be understood that not all packaged programs will suit the needs of all learners even in one school. Without thoughtful introduction and deliberate usage of these resources, we may well fall into the second sin of coverage beyond all else.

With this background in mind, let's begin to work through the process of determining our real curriculum needs under the big purpose umbrella and how we can apply the Triple P framework to guide our thinking.

Triple P Funnel

At this point we will begin working through the Triple P questions by funneling through the big idea questions about managing waste. We can ask ourselves: What kinds of waste occur within our decision-making process while determining our curriculum pieces? How much time are we wasting as we plan and go through materials that don't end up giving us depth for our students? How much energy are we using unnecessarily as we plan with others when our ideas and understandings of the purpose of our curriculum differ? In Figure 4.2, we begin a walkthrough of Triple P questions to help you sift through the bottom of the funnel, where we will pare down to essentials.

We can begin by examining the mental exhaustion that is often associated with reading through curriculum. This mental pressure can cause intellectual drain, pushing teachers into perpetual emotions of angst and confusion, particularly when there are changes in curriculum. Keep our goal in mind and determine the true purpose of the curriculum and resources that we use in our planning to begin the release of mental clutter. There are a variety of influences when it comes to identifying your purpose, shown in Figure 4.3. Depending on your particular context, these influences may include federal or state curriculum, your school district, the mission and vision of your school, as well as your own pedagogical standpoint. All of these influences need to be acknowledged and identified when considering the purpose of our curriculum and supporting resources. Through clarification of our purpose or overarching goal, we can begin to declutter, identify our priorities, and be able to pare down.

Figure 4.2

Curriculum Triple P Questions and Decision Making

Intellectual, Mental, Time, and Resource Waste

UPPER FUNNEL: PURPOSE

What is the purpose of our curriculum?

What are the factors influencing our purpose in our curriculum materials?

School-chosen: Do I understand the extent to which the lessons cover the standards and offer varied student engagement opportunities?

Teacher-created: In what ways does our unique curriculum enable us to meet the needs of our school community?

Overarching Priorities

What are the priorities within our curriculum?

What are the essentials I need to teach, and how do I ensure my priorities are met?

Have we clearly paced the year to cover the key standards, skills, and concepts?

How can we create a curriculum and design learning experiences that are meaningful and capture interest yet still meet our priorities without getting bogged down in the "things" of the program?

MIDDLE FUNNEL: PRIORITIES

Focused Priorities

How have we prioritized meeting student needs and interests based on the program?

Which pieces are essential to help students meet their grade benchmarks?

Which elements allow us to teach conceptually and develop transferable skills and attitudes?

BOTTOM FUNNEL: PARE DOWN

What can I pare down in my curriculum?

What is the best system to sift through programs and online resources in order to identify my curriculum materials?

How do I make this a sustainable practice?

Have we pared down to key priorities, essential concepts, skills, and standards?

Have we ensured balance in paring down resources so students have plenty of opportunities for engagement and challenge?

PARED DOWN TO ESSENTIALS

Figure 4.3

The Influences Impacting the Purpose of the Curriculum

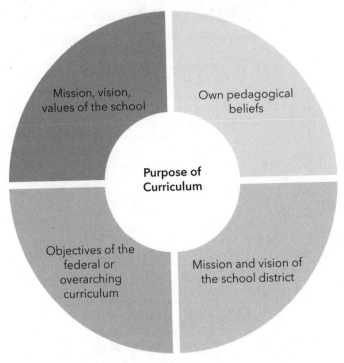

Once you have clarified your purpose, you will continue that care when you examine your priorities in order to begin paring down pieces of the curriculum. Instead of getting bogged down with fun yet not essential curriculum clutter during planning, we need to be thoughtful as we continue to question where our priorities lie. Funneling allows us to slow down and be intentional when choosing our focused priorities. It is not possible to prioritize everything and expect that the funnel will actually narrow our focus and support paring down the way it's intended. Let's pinpoint your funneled priorities to help you pare down. You may be able to identify your priorities, yet perhaps they are currently not being met. Let's look at Figure 4.4 to see an example of what we can bring to the table.

Figure 4.5 will get you started on your decluttering process and ask some deeper questions to help you with your decision making.

Now that you have considered these few questions, have you pinpointed your key elements? Have you noticed that perhaps you keep returning to student needs and engagement that is based on concepts and skills through teaching and learning experiences? The Triple P question funnel holds a whole gamut of questions and is a helpful tool to siphon out the nonessential

Figure 4.4
Middle Funnel Priorities

Area to Prioritize	Next Steps to Consider
Have we prioritized student needs?	• Consider the specific needs of both the whole group and individuals to ensure accessibility for all. • Speak with colleagues (curriculum developers, learning support, ELL teachers, etc.) to adapt and find access points.
Have we incorporated student interests?	• Elicit student input via votes, surveys, and questionnaires. • Postpone final planning until you have gotten to know your students.
Have we identified essentials in meeting benchmarks?	• Consider your vertical alignment across the school: what will be new content, and what is a review? • Make use of pre-assessments to highlight key areas for your cohort.
Do we have a clear pacing outline?	• Consider the year as a whole from the beginning. • Check that all essential standards have ample time across the year.
Have we considered concepts, skills, and attitudes?	• Refer to "double whammy" to support planning (p. 78).

Figure 4.5
Example Priority Flow Chart: Meeting Specific Student Needs

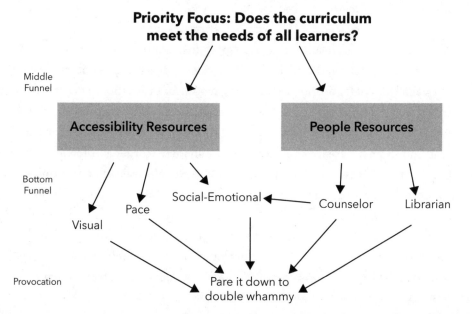

Priority Focus: Does the curriculum meet the needs of all learners?

elements of your curriculum. Other pieces are not necessarily unimportant, but they are not essential in sticking to your purpose and meeting your priorities.

Provocations to Sustain Your Decluttered Curriculum

Aligning Time with Priorities

Angela Watson, productivity and mindset specialist, discusses the idea of aligning how you spend your time with your priorities in her book *Fewer Things, Better* (2019). This does not mean that all your time gets spent on priorities and nothing else. Instead, ensure that your priorities do get sufficient time allocation and that they are not pushed aside for elements that do not serve your priorities. For example, if you have identified that your immediate priority in writing instruction for your students is on developing better word choice and vocabulary, and yet you are spending a significant portion of your literacy time each day on phonics activities, your time is not aligning with your identified priorities. How can we meet these identified priorities if we aren't dedicating a proportionate amount of our learning time to them? Once you have reflected upon what your priorities are, work toward building in enough time to meet that need.

The Question of Slow Schools

In her book *Cultivating Curiosity in K–12 Classrooms: How to Promote and Sustain Deep Learning* (2016), Wendy Ostroff discusses the idea of creating slow schools where we allow time and space in order to develop the soft skills so important in today's world. She discusses in depth the negative aspects of overfilled, oversubscribed teaching time on both teachers and students. Instead, she argues that unstructured schedules, where there is a reduced impetus to rush through content, will develop many of the important skills that will support creative, curious, and engaged learners. Allowing more time to invest in deeper thinking and exploration of ideas and questions will support the development of executive functioning skills, agency, cognition, responsibility, imagination, and creativity. Significantly, Ostroff tells us that "rushing is not the path to deep learning" (p. 110). Slowing down our curriculum expectations will support the development of true lifelong learners who will be capable of the types of skills and citizenship attributes that we need from the next generation. Paring down our curriculums to the essential skills, understandings, and concepts may allow us to slow down the frenetic pace and develop a deeper culture of learning.

Double Whammy

Guy Claxton (2018) discusses the idea of a split-screen approach to instruction in a blog post titled "Learning Friendly Teacher Action and Talk." Other educators have called this the "double whammy" of learning experiences. Using the double whammy approach involves recognizing that students are simultaneously learning the content as well as a learning behavior or skill. This means that while learning the curriculum, students are also learning transferable skills they need as learners. Claxton also points out that this development of learning behaviors will happen, regardless of whether this was intentionally planned.

Ask yourself

- How can I become more aware of the learning and school behaviors that I am unconsciously teaching alongside the content of my lesson?
- Can I explicitly plan for both the requirements of the curriculum *and* the soft skills that we know are so important in our ever-changing world?

This can be a simple change to make. It can be done quite seamlessly when you go back to think about your purpose and priorities. We are not adding on additional values programs or study skills initiatives, as those skills are already built in each and every session of the day. Most schools already have a set of learner attributes, dispositions, or characteristics in place that they wish their students to develop. What we can do, then, is take into account which one suits the content that we have planned and make a note of it with the content description. Let's say that Darius really wants to get the best "bang for his buck" in every single experience he plans for the day. This can become part of his routine with a simple reusable or laminated checklist that you can use for a quick reference as shown in Figure 4.6. The example shows a very close look at specific content standards that are directly connected to a concept, skill, or disposition. Keep in mind that you will plan this at the unit level. You can create your own table to keep alongside or within your unit planner that houses your targeted standards, concepts, skills, and dispositions. We do advise you to keep it simple!

Figure 4.6

Examples of Double Whammy or Split Screen

Content Strand and/or Standard	Concepts (C), Skills (S), Dispositions (D)
National Council for Social Studies (NCSS) Standard: 2e. Demonstrate an understanding that people in different times and places view the world differently.	C: Racism S: Critical thinking D: Empathy
NCSS Standard: 3f. Describe and speculate about *physical system* changes, such as seasons, climate and weather, and the water cycle.	C: Systems change S: Critical thinking D: Curiosity
Common Core Learning Standards for Mathematics: Practice Standard 1. Make sense of problems and persevere in solving them. Operations & Algebraic Thinking (2.OA) 1. Use addition and subtraction within 100 to solve one- and two-step word problems involving situations of adding to, taking from, putting together, taking apart, and comparing, with unknowns in all positions (e.g., by using drawings and equations with a symbol for the unknown number to represent the problem).	C: Number S: Self-management D: Perseverance

If we hand out a worksheet and tell the students the instructions for all activities of the sheet, we teach them that they can be passive and receive instructions for how to proceed. If we shush students' questions because we know we are going to run out of time to get this done, we are teaching them that their curiosity or search for clarification is not as important as the material and timing that we have decided for them. This practice negates your priority and likely adds stress in planning and preparation time.

Teaching Thinking

Teaching critical, creative, and logical thinking is one of the most important aspects of teaching for meaning in education. Building in strategic thinking routines and structures will support longevity and depth in your curriculum that you can use across content. In the next chapter, we will examine three schools of thought based on the research of John Hattie, David Hyerle, and Edward de Bono.

Wrapping It All Together with Claudia

Now that we have unraveled the multiple "what's" at play in our classrooms, let's examine this deconstruction of ideas that Claudia has created to increase her clarity of recognition and understanding of the purpose of curriculum at her school. Claudia teaches 2nd grade in Portland, Oregon. She has been feeling overwhelmed with the amount of content that she needs to teach in math throughout the year. Toward the end of the year, her team begins discussing an upcoming unit in which they will practice the times tables with the students. Her team members share ideas of how to practice this through engaging activities like singing songs, making artistic posters to take home, and playing team games. But Claudia is confused. Her school follows the Common Core State Standards, and she is pretty sure that rote learning times tables is not a part of the required content for 2nd grade. She asks her team about this, and they respond that they do it to help prepare the students for their work in 3rd grade and to give them a head start on what will be assessed in that year. So Claudia goes away to consider her purpose and priorities. Using the Triple P funnel, she reflects first on the purpose before filtering through to her and her students' priorities. In Figure 4.7, she takes into account all the different factors influencing this decision.

Claudia carefully weighs up the mission and vision statements from each of these stakeholders. As she filters through these different considerations through her curriculum funnel, she can't see any evidence that it would be necessary to prep students for the year ahead or that the purpose of instruction in 2nd grade is to get ready for 3rd grade. She recognizes the positive intentions from her colleagues, but she decides to use this time instead to review the math concepts already covered throughout the year and practice their transfer and application in creative ways. Claudia chooses to pare down and use a double whammy in order to meet the priorities of the students in her room rather than adding onto an already crowded curriculum.

Figure 4.7
Claudia's Triple P Upper Funnel Thinking

Missions and Visions	Focus Statement
Own Philosophy	I believe that all children are unique and have something special that they can bring to their own education. I will assist my students to express themselves and accept themselves for who they are, as well as embrace the differences of others.
School Level	In Grade 2, instructional time should focus on four critical areas: (1) extending understanding of base-ten notation, (2) building fluency with addition and subtraction, (3) using standard units of measure, and (4) describing and analyzing shapes.
School District	School Mission Statement: We are a diverse community of life-long learners who are creative, responsible, and respectful. We are committed to meeting the academic, social, and emotional needs of our students.
State/Federal Curriculum	A graduate of Portland Public Schools will be a compassionate critical thinker, able to collaborate and solve problems, and prepared to lead a more socially just world.

In Conclusion

Chapter Takeaways

- Your curriculum tells you what to teach, not who or how.
- Always align the purpose of the curriculum with the priority.
- Find the essentials from your resources, like concepts and transferrable strategies.
- Choose materials and resources that support depth.

Lingering Question

Now that I have pared down my curriculum resources (and distractions), how will I teach for depth?

Up Next

In Chapter 5, we will be digging into the "how" of teaching: instruction and assessment. We have paired these two aspects of teaching because you cannot have one without the other! After you spend time filtering through your curriculum, you may want to proceed to the next chapter and begin Triple P-ing your instructional and assessment practices.

5

Decluttering Instructional and Assessment Strategies

The Problem: Too Many Ways to Teach So Much Content

From the moment we start learning about teaching, we are introduced to a multitude of strategies to help us make learning and assessing worthwhile, engaging, and exciting for our students. A simple teacher reflection or internet search will reveal a never-ending stream of ideas and suggestions about how we can use these strategies to amplify our teaching and make the most of our time with our students. Different strategies could be identified disparately: traditional versus progressive strategies, according to different teaching styles, summative and/or formative assessments, personalized versus collaborative versus whole-group strategies. But how do we select from these strategies to teach and assess in a way that matches our authentic selves as teachers and the needs of our students without driving ourselves crazy trying a million different approaches? We only have roughly six hours a day with our students, so knowing how to make good choices in our strategy and assessment use can feel overwhelming. English teacher, head of learning and research at Wellington College, and author Carl Hendrick discusses how a lot of what is happening in our classrooms is not a good use of our time, and instead we need to cut down what we are doing to just the best possible strategies. In an article on The Guardian.com, he states that "[o]ften, these approaches not only have limited impact on student learning but can have a hugely detrimental impact on teacher workload and well-being" (Hendrick, 2017).

The Cycle Elements for Instruction and Assessment Decluttering

Act. In this chapter, you will continue decluttering, although there is a shift in the type of waste you are decluttering. The decluttering process here is focused around intellectual, mental, and time waste.

*Note: You may find yourself doing some additional inquiring and investigating into some of the research behind mental fatigue and burnout, as well as other elements of the mental decluttering process.

If you have already worked through the process of decluttering your curriculum in Chapter 4, that's a great start. Now focus on how you can thoughtfully plan your instructional practices for rich and meaningful learning. Before you begin working through this next chapter, we would like to preface the work ahead with a deep breath. You may be questioning our intent of a "minimalism in teaching" book at the moment! While we are certain we *have* written a book about paring back your teaching practice, we also have to do the diligent deep digging and spend time laying out each element to carefully evaluate all of its pieces. The intent is that we are supporting you with some background on the minimalist mindset and to highlight and embrace this initial learning and habit recreation. This is about a change in your teaching lifestyle and your instructional practice as your essential daily cuppa. Teaching is a huge part of our lives and our identities. This process is a set of uncomfortable habit changes, yet we hope you remember that you have a little nest with us. We support the work you are embarking on and want you to declutter your teaching life. Now let's move along to what we would consider the most impactful element of teaching and learning—something you perhaps have been anticipating. So here we go!

Refocusing on Instruction

With almost any life situation, it is easy for us to focus on the what because what questions are fairly straightforward to answer.

- What is the problem here?
- What is bothering you?
- What is causing stress?
- What are you teaching?

Make no mistake—we are not saying easy-to-answer questions are easy to solve or that they make us feel warm, cozy, and accomplished. A challenging part of moving through this process is to first decide on your curriculum (your what), and shifting to the application (your how) is the juicy part. How much time do we actually spend thinking through the how that follows these what's?

- How will I solve the problem?
- How will I reduce the stress of this?
- How will I teach this?

We must now filter through the instructional and assessment practices to ensure they will match with your newly pared-down curriculum. Determining your instructional and assessment practices based on your curriculum does not mean the decisions you make must be complicated or that you need to use every kind of research-based strategy in the teacher toolkit. It means you are digging deeper into practices that will enrich the learning experiences you present to your students using your pared-down curricula file. This is where we set up your bank of go-to strategies that will translate across content and discipline.

Let's take a moment and revisit the types of waste that we discussed earlier and consider this as the top of our Triple P funnel as we begin to sift through instruction and assessment practices before we head into the decision-making processes.

Triple P Funneling

Now we can begin our focused thinking as we work through the lens of the Triple P funnel. How can we find our purpose, priorities, and opportunities to pare down when planning and implementing our instructional strategies? When we speak of instructional practices, we are also speaking of assessment practices inclusively. We view assessment practices as an integral part of the instructional cycle. If we are striving to minimize our work as educators and streamline our approach, it makes sense to closely interconnect and coordinate our instruction and assessment practices. Planning for them as separate entities will only add time waste and mental fatigue. However, we will address certain aspects of assessment separately within our provocations section in order to get more specific.

Before we begin funneling, consider a few top funnel questions related to the waste you will be evaluating: What is my biggest source of waste within the instruction and assessment processes that happen in my classroom? Am I frivolously wasting energy devising assessments that don't end up showing us the data we need? Am I expending too much emotional energy when I plan with others who have different understandings of how to use instructional time? See Figure 5.1 to see some examples of where you can reduce some of this energy and use it in more efficient ways.

The upper funnel of instruction and assessment is your overarching purpose, as we have established in previous chapters. Generally, the purpose of your instruction will be clear to you, yet it can become clouded with so much interfering clutter. For support, we have provided a long list of purposes for instruction and assessment in Appendix B. Let's consider some purpose questions and then further dissect your priorities.

The most fundamental element here will be to establish what your purpose is within your instruction and assessment choices. Being clear and concise in your choice will assist you in making faster decisions about your priorities and what can be pared down. Here we will enlist the help of Jay McTighe and Willis's (2019) categorization of goals from *Upgrade Your Teaching: UbD Meets Neuroscience*. In order to clarify our purpose, slow your process and consider just one learning session at a time. To find your purpose in instruction, use the sentence provided in the list on page 88 and make use of it for a recent or upcoming learning experience (remembering that you may want to double whammy your session and include both elements, described in Chapter 4).

Figure 5.1

Instruction and Assessment Triple P Questions and Decision Making

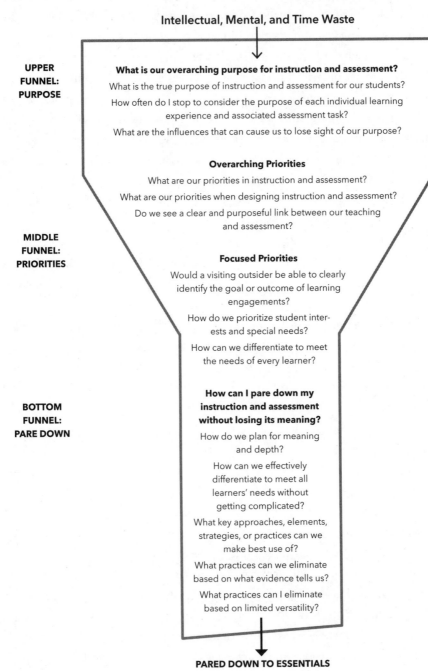

Intellectual, Mental, and Time Waste

UPPER FUNNEL: PURPOSE

What is our overarching purpose for instruction and assessment?

What is the true purpose of instruction and assessment for our students?

How often do I stop to consider the purpose of each individual learning experience and associated assessment task?

What are the influences that can cause us to lose sight of our purpose?

Overarching Priorities

What are our priorities in instruction and assessment?

What are our priorities when designing instruction and assessment?

Do we see a clear and purposeful link between our teaching and assessment?

MIDDLE FUNNEL: PRIORITIES

Focused Priorities

Would a visiting outsider be able to clearly identify the goal or outcome of learning engagements?

How do we prioritize student interests and special needs?

How can we differentiate to meet the needs of every learner?

BOTTOM FUNNEL: PARE DOWN

How can I pare down my instruction and assessment without losing its meaning?

How do we plan for meaning and depth?

How can we effectively differentiate to meet all learners' needs without getting complicated?

What key approaches, elements, strategies, or practices can we make best use of?

What practices can we eliminate based on what evidence tells us?

What practices can I eliminate based on limited versatility?

PARED DOWN TO ESSENTIALS

The purpose of this learning session is to support students to

- Gain knowledge of . . . .
- Build the skill of . . . .
- Develop understanding of . . . .
- Transfer their knowledge of . . . .

Completing this sentence may also create a clearer connection between your instructional strategies and assessment, and how they can translate across disciplines. The more we can declutter this, the clearer your vision can be in paring down on strategies.

Here's an example. Charise and her grade team have recently been laser-focused on having a clear purpose and established set of priorities in their reading sessions with their 7th grade students in which they focus on Common Core English Language Arts Reading Standard 7.2: determine a theme, analyze its development, and then present an objective summary of different texts (this is the what). They decided they would give this a double whammy approach to teaching by collaborating with the content specialist teachers to ensure that students were reading some content material in reading classes. Here's what they came up with: "Our 7th grade reading students will *transfer their knowledge* of theme to different genres and types of text."

Once they filled in the statement, they then needed to ensure that their priorities were going to be met within their groups.

After you have carefully evaluated your purpose and begun the process of identifying and sorting through your priorities, we will continue funneling and examining more focused priorities in order to begin paring down pieces of your instruction. In this space, we have to also consider priorities for each child's learning needs, so the process can become quite granular.

To do this, we have to think about how our instruction practices provide transferable use yet provide scaffolds within them for students. This is not more work but, rather, differentiated and strategic. By being intentional, we can combat intellectual and mental exhaustion as we use the Triple P process. Read through the questions on the next page and tune into which you need to focus on, and then we can head to the next step.

Once a clear statement about the purpose is established for your chosen instructional practices, you will be able to make more deliberate decisions about what the priority should be within your planning and what extraneous elements can be pared away. When Charise and her team reconvened, they determined that they would really need to expose students to a variety of reading materials of interest in which they would be able to identify themes. They were excited to be able to have students read from a number of genres and content areas. This is the time to consider which research-based practices will help you reach the goal for the learning sessions.

As you work through this similar exercise, use the thinking around the questions in Figure 5.1 and ask yourself

- What key approaches, elements, strategies, or practices can I make use of?
- What practices can I eliminate based on what evidence tells me?
- What practices can I eliminate based on limited versatility?

Take a moment to think about your guiding statement. The following sentence prompts will be helpful to filter through your priorities and eliminate those that are not. You can visit Appendix B for lists of purposes and priorities of instruction and assessment to help you find your focal points.

- The purpose of this session is to support students to. . . .
- The research-based practices I can prioritize are. . . .
- The instructional and assessment strategies I can eliminate are. . . .

Considering instructional practices at this specific level is a challenging cognitive task. We advise working on this process with your team and discussing your thoughts with each other so you can get to why you arrive at the decisions you make for your instruction, why you've chosen certain priorities, and why you've pared down particular elements.

Provocations to Sustain Decluttered Instructional and Assessment Practices

When considering ways in which we can work toward a more minimalist approach to our instructional and assessment strategies, two branches of thought begin to emerge. These two branches encompass the different approaches you can take in the instructional strategies you use and the different implementation strategies that strive for a more minimalist experience. The approaches you choose outline the different pedagogical approaches that make the most of your time with your students. The implementation section outlines different planning and procedural tools you can use to help make your teaching life more succinct, organized, and robust.

Decluttering Strategy Approaches

John Hattie (2009) and his team have spent years at the University of Auckland and the University of Melbourne collecting, collating, and reviewing analysis of educational research. He regularly updates the list of influences and effect sizes related to student achievement, and his most recently updated list is based on more than 1,200 meta-analyses. This important work allows us to cut through the myriad of ideas and conjectures in education and focus on what we *know* to be impactful. If we can witness from this work that giving feedback is more effective than providing worked examples, or that scaffolding has a larger effect size than ability grouping, surely the onus is on us as educators to make use of this information. Having said that, let's look at some of these approaches.

Power Tools

In *Powerful Teaching: Unleash the Science of Learning*, Agarwal and Bain (2019) outline four "power tools" to ensure that teaching is of a high standard. These tools are based on a large body of research by cognitive scientists about how we learn best. The power tools they outline are

1. Retrieval practice ("reaching back" for encoded information).
2. Spacing (leaving time between retrieval practice events).
3. Interleaving (weaving content together during practice events).
4. Feedback-driven metacognition (recognizing what you know and what you don't).

The authors outline why and how using these practices will ensure our teaching is most impactful for our students. Why not use these high-level ways of thinking with students? If we can inform ourselves about the tools to make the most of our limited time with our students, this should surely be the way forward. We cannot play guessing games with the education of our students.

Teaching Thinking

Let's revisit this idea of teaching thinking. In the previous chapter, we gave you a little peek at the connection between the school of teaching thinking and the relationship to a school's purpose and priorities. Building on that now, below we have named some of the thinking development exercises created by each researcher. These tools allow you to focus your teaching on how students can use visual organizers for the development of their own cognition, rather than teach with a collection using only things that may end up cluttering your instructional practices rather than enhancing them. These cognitive routines and visual maps are malleable and simple without sacrificing the intricate nature of thinking. Understanding these frameworks do require some pedagogical investment on the behalf of teachers and more cognitive exercises in teacher planning, which in turn can result in higher levels of student thinking and understanding overall.

Develop Curiosity, Buy-In, and Agency

One of the fastest ways to declutter instructional strategies is to work hard at developing students who are curious, engaged, and taking ownership over their learning. Wendy Ostroff (2016) said, "Teaching and learning are never a chore" when students are intrinsically motivated (p. 3), so as much as you can, hand over the education to the students, and you will be rewarded with students who are interested and motivated.

Here are some key takeaways to develop intrinsic motivation for learning:

- Encourage student choice as much as possible.
- Allow space for students to follow their interests.
- Be adaptable where necessary.
- Encourage responsibility for the learning space and the learning itself.
- Support the development of democratic processes in your classroom.
- Explore avenues for student voice.
- Make the goals of learning explicit.

The transference of responsibility from teacher to student can make your instruction more meaningful and much less cluttered. How might the development of student agency look in your classroom?

Decluttering Strategy Implementation

Create Buffers

Returning now to Geoff McKeown (2014) and his work in *Essentialism: The Disciplined Pursuit of Less*, we will explore one of his strategies for essentialists. McKeown discusses the importance of creating buffers to avoid underestimating how much time it takes to complete tasks or achieve your learning goal.

As we know, school hours are precious, and it is common for teachers to feel like they are rushed to get through all the requirements of the curriculum. This can be because we are dealing with students who are complex humans whose learning is unpredictable. While we may not be able to pare down the content we need to cover in the curriculum, we can make the effort to ensure buffers are in place to protect our priorities. These buffers can take many different forms, but they are usually elements within our planning documents.

Consider this example. Fridays are a classic day for scheduled buffer time. Teacher planning schedules may have some Friday time allocated to "golden time" or "ketchup and mustard time," in which teachers allow themselves and their students the time to complete tasks that may not have been finished during the week. Scheduling this time means we do not need to focus on the stress of having unfinished work, nor do we need to get tangled in catching up our absentees because we have built in the buffer. We know there is always that extra time there to finish off, go back, or recoup. The added bonus of this particular buffer is that when students are finished with their tasks, they have self-directed time that allows them to design, create, research, or whatever falls within those parameters. The added bonus is that this time for student autonomy will support our priorities and enable us to keep pared down to our original plan—no additional planning yet additional meaningful learning time. And it's always fantastic to see what they come up with when allowed to direct themselves!

A second example to consider when contemplating another effective way to ensure buffers are included is to allow for "unplanned" time at the end of each term, semester, or academic year. This buffer may only be a week in length, but it allows for time and space to accommodate any units of work that may have been pushed back or elongated throughout the teaching period.

Does this situation sound familiar? Your unit on narrative writing was supposed to finish last Friday, but students require more time to complete their science research. So your narrative writing summative task remains unfinished, and now starting the next persuasive writing unit until Thursday will not be realistic. Think about how much less overwhelmed you would feel if you planned in a week buffer at the end of term allowing for writing unit spillover time. Placing buffers in your yearly plans will reduce the tension and pressure of covering the whole curriculum within your teaching year. Edmonton Public Schools High School mathematics teacher, Jodi Mykula, plans three-day buffers at the end of her units to ensure students are prepared for their summative assessments. If she sees the students need the time to clarify misconceptions and have additional questions answered, she uses the extra buffer days to address those.

One Teaching Point

"Now hang on! A moment ago, you were telling us to double whammy our learning sessions, and now you're telling us to focus on one teaching point? Make up your mind!"

You are absolutely right. This does sound like a contradiction. When we talk about maintaining one teaching point, we ask you to think about how important it is to have a clear focus on the objective of each lesson, rather than spreading it too broadly and losing the true meaning of what we aim to achieve. It can be easy to get caught in the whirlwind when attempting to address many skills and attitudes based on your content, as we have shown, so proceed with caution. Let's explore the following example to illustrate what we mean.

Andrew is teaching his 4th grade class how to write exciting leads for narratives. He has three different examples from books to share and has also created a self-assessment checklist for students to use independently to ensure they maintain focus as they write. When his lesson begins, he reviews what narrative texts are and elicits a discussion about the differences between narrative and information texts. He shows the first example text, which illustrates how to start a story with a sound. The second example illustrates how to begin with an action, and the third with dialogue. The students turn and talk to discuss what they might like to write about today. Andrew then shares the checklists and discusses how to use them before sending the students off to get started. This writing session would likely end up with a jumble of questions from students. So what *was* the focus of this lesson? So many questions arise!

- Was it the features of narrative texts?
- Was it the difference between narrative and information texts?
- Was it how to start a story with a sound? Or an action? Or with dialogue?

- Was it the importance of rehearsing your writing before starting?
- Was it how to use a checklist?
- Or was it the need to be reflective about your work as a writer?

How would you know? And more important, how would the students know? While each individual aspect of this session is valid, the end result of putting them all in one session is a congested, puzzling writing lesson. Keeping our sessions focused on one point will enable us to clearly plan for our teaching as well as keep the true intention of learning clear for our students. It will also help us monitor for the topic of the following section: cognitive load theory.

Cognitive Load

Sumeracki et al. (2018) outline some of the key research about cognitive load, or overload, the theory that our brains can only process so much information at a time. We receive plentiful information each day, but a lot of it is discarded, as our working memories can only store so much. This is an important idea for educators to grapple with because we do not want to over-saturate our students with information that is not going to be remembered or processed each day, or even each learning session. It is essential to find the right level of challenge and interest without dousing our students with too much wasted information. This is where it becomes necessary to focus your teaching points. Focusing on a single teaching point paired with a key learning disposition will help you prioritize for each learning session. Yes, other things may pop up during the session, but with this priority clearly articulated, you will be able to keep cycling back to the key focus and keep the learning experience on point. As a result, this should help us focus on what student learning we are monitoring and measuring, resulting in a clear and focused assessment for learning.

Educational Technology in Your Planning and Preparation

Educational technology has expanded exponentially since the early 2010s. Because of the deluge of tools and gadgets that can slow our process of decluttering, we will keep this section pared down. We suggest using tools that your school already has chosen; however, we know that teachers love to explore applications on devices as much as the students do! When you learn of an amazing app that potentially supports something you want your students to work on, go ahead and play with it. Then refocus and give some thought to the value and purpose of what you are about to create (harness the thoughts you had earlier in the chapter when reading about the Pinterest classroom). If a creation tool allows you to make something, provides a multiple-time use, and supports the learning of your students once you present it to them, then consider using it as one of your go-to tools.

For example, if you want to use a document creation tool to whip up your own modified version of some visible thinking routines or for a versatile checklist for writing, go for it. Do be cautious to correlate the purpose behind this tool, and ensure that it does not limit your students' ability to show their thinking and learning. You also need to think back to your priority (students and their learning) and ensure that the strategies you choose in your instruction will suit the students in your current classroom. Be sure that you do not let this creation time be one of the ditches that you get stuck in, kicking yourself later that you spent time preparing things you ended up not using or needing.

A Synthesis of Provocations

Spending the time to sift through the aspects of instruction in terms of approach and implementation allows us now to synthesize and examine what we have pared down. We do hope that the way we have chunked out the pieces of instruction have made it manageable to digest and think about with intention. This process is intended to make the best sense possible for your context and teaching life. See an example in Figure 5.2.

Assessment

Are you excited to move along into the assessment piece? We hope you're feeling some momentum as you read and work through the framework! Please remember that our intent is for you to eventually gain a sense of lightness from the heaviness that can make us feel like we are packed down. As you read through the previous section on using power-packed practices for less time and intellectual waste, you may have been thinking about how you would assess your students within these rich experiences. Depth in learning provides a multitude of opportunities for embedded assessment. How's that, you ask?

Figure 5.2

Pared-Down Provocations in Action

Pared-Down Examples of Unit Planning	Instructional Practices to Meet Your Purposes and Priorities
Science Concepts • Matter • Structure • Energy • Space **Skills** • Observation • Questioning **Dispositions** • Inquisitiveness • Resourcefulness	**Visible Thinking Routines** • Zoom in (or modify to your own zoom out) • See, think, wonder • Think, puzzle, explore **Visual Tools for Thinking** • Brainstorm webs • Graphic organizers for analyzing ideas • Concept maps
Social Sciences Concepts • Organizations • Systems **Skills** • Speaking • Listening **Dispositions** • Empathy • Thoughtfulness	**Six Thinking Hats (de Bono): Six "Thinking Hats" to Section Thinking** • White hat = facts • Yellow hat = positives • Black hat = judgment or devil's advocate • Red hat = emotions and hunches • Green hat = creativity • Blue hat = thinking process manager
Citizenship Concepts • Equality • Diversity • Responsibility **Skills** • Speaking • Listening • Critical Thinking **Dispositions** • Tolerance • Patience	**Cognitive/Experiential Practices and Protocols** • Matching • Identifying patterns • Sorting and classifying • Object inquiries • Debate • Socratic seminar • Discussion circles • Liberating structure protocols **Power Tools** • Reaching back • Spacing • Interleaving • Feedback-driven metacognition
Mathematics Concepts • Numbers • Patterns • Shape and Space **Skills** • Analyzing • Observation • Problem solving **Dispositions** • Logic • Independent thinking	**Student Agency** • Engage student interest • Autonomy in learning and creation of product **Educational Technology** • Collaboration platforms such as G Suite or Google Classroom • Versatile creation tools such as the built-in notes apps on your phone • Flipgrid or Padlet for immediate feedback, student voice, and agency

Let's revisit our Triple P framework at the upper funnel level in Figure 5.3 and look through an assessment lens.

Figure 5.3
Purpose of Assessment Flow

What is the purpose of my assessment?

Is it to drive instruction and ensure students engage with what they need to practice and learn?

Or is it to ensure you are reporting and grading accurately so that it is a true reflection of achievement?

The purpose of your assessment and the role it plays in our work needs to be kept in focus. It must match your priorities, and it must remain pared down. We can get some help in answering our overarching question: What is my purpose in teaching and learning? Going back to *Upgrade Your Teaching* (2019) with Jay McTighe and Judy Willis, we can reflect on the importance and central role of establishing goals. Thoughtful creation of goals will help us and our students focus the aim, or purpose, of our assessment. They outline four different types of goals:

- Goals related to knowledge.
- Goals related to skills and processes.
- Goals related to understanding.
- Goals related to transfer.

We can find a clearer path to the purpose of our assessment pieces through clear examination of our goal. If we have designed a unit of work to encourage the transfer and application of the learning but then only assess the knowledge built, we have moved away from the purpose of the designed unit.

Take a moment here to think about this example: Wes receives his graded English essay about the symbolism in *Macbeth*, and written across the top is a single comment about the quality of his handwriting with one mark removed for illegibility. Some questions immediately come to our minds.

- How does this feedback and grading reflect the purpose of the assignment?
- What impact will this type of assessment feedback have on Wes's learning and future achievement?
- How is this indicative of the teacher's priorities in class?

In *Innovate Inside the Box* (2019), authors George Couros and Katie Novak urge us to move away from the human-less letter and number grades that are often associated with data and assessment and instead consider being learner-driven and evidence-informed. Considering assessment strategies and approaches in this way changes our focus back to our real purpose in education: the development of our students. Unbalanced focus on grades, percentages, or projected growth targets may reduce our students to little more than statistics. We will readily admit that rifling through data can be interesting, rewarding, and informative. But if we let that override the depth of contextual knowledge we have about our students, then we may have lost sight of both the purpose and priority of our work as educators.

Developing Self-Assessment Practices

You know you can teach your students to assess themselves, right? This is an immensely responsible teacher habit to build into your instructional and assessment practices if you haven't already. This is in part because of something Dylan Wiliam has researched and shared with educators. In his article "The Secret of Effective Feedback" (2016), Wiliam wrote that "[t]he amount of feedback we can give our students is limited. In the longer term, the most productive strategy is to develop our students' ability to give themselves feedback." Teaching students to assess themselves is a skill set they can use throughout their lives. Think about how you know if you are behaving or acting within the parameters of your role as a student on the playground, as a college student, or at your job. Do we wait for someone to give feedback on everything? No, we intrinsically seek ways to determine if we are on track. That's what we want from our students in their academic roles as well. We want them to use their skill sets that we have been teaching with purpose and a focused set of priorities so that they, too, can pare down the clutter around them and find or create techniques to improve whatever they create. Take advantage of teaching even the youngest students some age-appropriate techniques that you use when you assess them yourself.

- **Simple checklists:** We use to-do checklists all the time in everyday life (maybe not to the best of their intended uses, but that's for another book), but there is some merit in teaching students the benefits of creating and using one consistently. Why not have students be involved in creating simple and versatile checklists that can be used to help them (and you) track elements addressed on their tasks or assignments?

- **Single-point rubrics:** When choosing assessments that are learner-driven, Jennifer Gonzalez (2014) shared the idea behind a single-point rubric on her blog CultofPedagogy.com, and since then, teachers have adopted this practice to improve the quality of their assessments and the feedback given to students. A single-point rubric is designed to keep the focus on just a small number of criteria in developing a product based on content and skills, with the feedback focused on the assignment's strong qualities and areas of needed improvement.

- **Feedback:** Feedback has a great impact on student learning. When you invest the time to teach your students to give constructive feedback, you meet your priorities to deepen learning and make it student-centered *and* pare down on how you spend your time. Sumeracki et al. (2018) also state, "Ultimately, it's best to give some feedback than none at all—and do not fret if you can't deliver it instantly" (p. 143). The key is that students receive feedback in some form, from someone, and are able to use it to make improvements.

- **Mind maps:** David Hyerle (2011) has stated that students can participate in the powerful process of self-assessing their thinking when they create a map of the thinking they have been doing over time. This may be a brainstorm web, a story outline, or a timeline of events. When students are given the autonomy to collect their thinking in a loosely framed map and revisit it after further learning has taken place, they become self-assessors.

Paring Back to What Counts

As we have mentioned previously, making use of research- and evidence-based practices is a key element to establishing your purpose, priorities, and most specifically how to pare down. How much time and effort are we wasting on trends in education that have no basis and rely more on solely anecdotal evidence than any real or significant data? A key principle when considering paring down is this: How can we use research, science, and data to get to the most useful and effective strategies in our instruction and assessment?

At this point, let's now examine two examples of how pared-down research-based instruction and assessment might look.

Angelique is working with her beginning English language learners and wants to develop their vocabulary around the months of the year because the students will soon be entering a time unit in their home classes. She follows a protocol for finding her purpose and comes up with a statement: "The purpose of this session is to support students to gain knowledge of English month vocabulary *while* building the skill of turn taking."

Now armed with this purpose, she can consider what her priorities are in planning and pare back what is unnecessary to meet this purpose. She will not worry about any crafting or competitive elements, as this will not meet her clear purpose. Instead, she will prioritize strategies in which students take turns to retrieve and rehearse the months of the year in English. She decides to make use of a quiz, quiz, trade strategy in order for students to retrieve vocabulary knowledge they may already have, gain immediate feedback on what they already know or do not know, and practice taking turns with each other.

While examining grade 9 history work samples, Yuri realizes that his students need further practice in identifying evidence to support the author's claim. He completes Figure 5.4 to consider his purpose, priorities, and how to pare down.

Yuri decides that the best way forward is for his students to reflectively work through work samples marked with his feedback. He will give time at the start of his next session for the students to review what they did well and where errors were made. They will then have a follow-up practice finding evidence in another text and summarizing their findings. He will ensure he includes further spaced practice over the next few weeks to keep this skill active.

If Yuri, and all teachers, can keep this one pared-down idea about assessment, we can sustainably make our practices meaningful and useful. And that has often been stated by Kath Murdoch (2020), Australian inquiry-based learning guru: "An assessment isn't worth doing if it doesn't improve student learning."

Figure 5.4

Yuri's Triple P Thinking

Research-based practices I can prioritize	The purpose of this session	Instructional and assessment strategies I can eliminate
• Feedback • Metacognition • Critical thinking • Summarizing • Spaced practice	Support students to build the skill of stating evidence from the text to support claims while being self-reflective about their learning.	• Returned work with zero feedback • Worked example of how it should have been answered • Static anchor chart on the wall referencing how to find evidence • Establishing ability groups or learning style groups to revise the work

In Conclusion

Chapter Takeaways

- Double whammy your instruction by simultaneously planning for both content and learner attributes.
- Focus your intention and reduce cognitive overload by ensuring you are aiming for just one teaching point in each lesson.
- Develop curiosity and agency in order to make the most of your instructional time.
- Assessment practices need to be reflective of the purpose of our overall work in education as well as each individual task.
- Enlist evidence-based practices in order to make best use of your instructional, assessment, and planning time.
- Be clear and mindful about the purpose of instruction and assessment to better prioritize and pare down.

Lingering Question

How is this all relevant for making meaning in learning for and with my students?

Up Next

In the next chapter, we will be looking at how all the focus we have invested into creating and being open to a minimalist mindset using the Triple P framework is really about making your teaching life richer by staying pared down. Chapter 6 is about advocating for depth in learning and bringing this relevant way of thinking to your students as life skills.

Advocating for Minimalism in Your Teaching Environment

The What and Why of Advocating to Be a Minimalist Teacher

First of all, we want to applaud your dedication to the process you have started and the work that you will do moving forward.

You've been working through the entire Triple P framework—the funnel questions, decision making, and the cycle—and you are at this stage of building awareness in shaping yourself into a minimalist teacher. This means raising awareness and perhaps sharing with others.

Throughout the book, we have been referencing how much waste results from our beloved field of teaching. We have invested our life's work in this essential service, this necessary profession, but it is one that needs a serious overhaul in how resources are used. So why are we doing this? Jane Goodall, famous chimpanzee researcher and activist, often says that every individual matters. Every individual has a role to play. Every individual makes a difference. So ask yourself

- Why do I want to make a difference?
- What do I want my difference to be?
- How can I make these important differences?

Our hope is that the difference that we all want to make in education—particularly after experiencing such educational pandemonium during a worldwide pandemic—is to create calm mental and physical spaces in which we can teach and students can learn. We want to make a difference in what we offer students and how we offer it. We want to really refocus ourselves on actually making a difference in the lives of students. But first, let's consider a few challenges that you may encounter in your quest to advocate in making your difference.

The Cycle Element for Your Advocacy Work

Advocate. In this chapter, your primary work is to advocate for this approach as a teaching life you believe.

*Note: You may find yourself continuing to declutter, although there is a shift in the type of waste you are decluttering. The decluttering process here is focused around intellectual, mental, and time waste.

Challenge #1: Getting Others to See the Value in Decluttering

When you look around, is anyone with you? If not, you can present the research, the connections to well-being, and the impact of our complicated relationship with waste.

Honesty alert! Adopting a minimalist approach to teaching is a messy task—at first, anyway. We assure you, though, that digging through the mess, sorting it out, and gaining a sense of clarity is worth it in the long run. When your colleagues see the benefits of your decluttering process and how you reevaluate spaces and resources, they will see the value in creating a pared-down teaching life. Think about the ultimate importance of this process. Our hope is that your chance of burning out lessens as you transform how you and your colleagues engage in systematic mass decluttering and think about what you need in order to offer meaningful learning experiences to your students. During this process we hope that we can help you to create sustainable teaching habits and share them with those around you.

Challenge #2: You're the Only One Ready

Are your colleagues unsure of your dedication to declutter your classroom, curriculum, and instruction? Once you get rolling, you might become a decluttering fanatic. You may want to drag your teammates along with you. Remember: becoming a minimalist teacher can sound extreme to those who are not ready to behold it. But you are ready. You are reading this book and have the ready mindset to take the plunge. You took a risk to move to a teaching approach you believe in. You know your purpose, you've aligned your priorities, and you are, or will be, pared down to create a teaching life that has depth and meaning and isn't lost in the clutter of it all. Don't be afraid to start the journey on your own!

Challenge #3: You Feel Stuck

Are you asking yourself, "I believe in this, I want to do this work, but how can I advocate for this approach when I feel stuck and I cannot get myself to take action with it?" It's OK. You are not alone. We are guessing there will be a group of our readers who ask themselves the same question. Because we thought you and others might run into a few hiccups, we have a thought web in Figure 6.1 to help you filter through how you can advocate for yourself as you embark on this road.

Triple P Framework for Advocacy

Obviously, part of our advocacy plan is to build your own advocacy plan in your endeavor ahead. So let's walk through the Triple P framework and begin tuning into the purpose, priorities, and paring-down process for your aim to advocate.

Purpose
- What is the purpose of advocating for a minimalist approach in my teaching life?

Figure 6.1
Suggestions for When You Feel Stuck

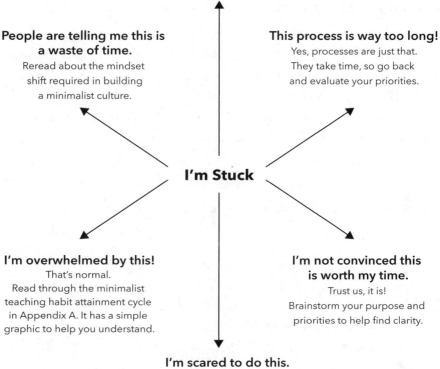

I feel alone and I don't have support in doing this.
This can be scary! Start advocating for others to join you and do a book study.

People are telling me this is a waste of time.
Reread about the mindset shift required in building a minimalist culture.

This process is way too long!
Yes, processes are just that. They take time, so go back and evaluate your priorities.

I'm Stuck

I'm overwhelmed by this!
That's normal.
Read through the minimalist teaching habit attainment cycle in Appendix A. It has a simple graphic to help you understand.

I'm not convinced this is worth my time.
Trust us, it is!
Brainstorm your purpose and priorities to help find clarity.

I'm scared to do this.
This is a normal reaction.
Reread the benefits this approach can have on your life!

- What is the purpose in trying to bring my team along in this process?
- What is the purpose in exposing students to this way of teaching and learning?

Priorities: What are the priorities I've set in becoming a minimalist teacher?
- In the physical environment
- In our school initiatives
- In our curriculum
- In my instruction
- In assessment

Pare Down

- How can I advocate to begin the process of paring down?
- How can I advocate to keep our prioritized areas pared down?

An Advocacy Audit

Before you ramp up your advocacy efforts, determine what you are already doing. Perhaps you work through the audit in Figure 6.2 to align priorities once you have decluttered. How can you use an advocacy audit to continue minimizing mental weariness, deplete clutter, and remain pared down? To do this, let's visit some key ideas from Couros and Novak (2019) about ways to bring about change in education.

1. Bring it back to the kids.
2. Model the change you want to see.
3. Show that you understand the value that already exists.
4. Share your stories.

Do these ideas sound familiar? We guess these ideas exist in your realm of thinking already but may have gotten buried under all the stuff of teaching. To help you recapture the importance of these key ideas, use the prompts in Figure 6.2 to think through ways to become a more minimalist educator.

- If you answer yes to any item, jot examples in the box to the right what you do to support minimalist teaching.
- If you choose no, jot down what you think your barriers might be in this part of your advocacy plan.

Remember that when you do this, you are considering ways in which you may or may not be advocating for minimalist teaching practices already.

Your Minimalist Teacher Advocacy Action Plan

Now that you have completed the audit, you can quickly see which "ways to change" you already advocate for, which you need to move along with, and how they are aligned. You can use the Advocacy Action Plan template in Figure 6.3 to organize your ideas.

Did you notice that your audit and action plan focused on people, resources, and time already in the realm of your teaching sphere? Did you add any "things" that you need with intention? Did you keep your focus on

Figure 6.2
Minimalist Teacher Advocacy Audit

Do I . . .	Y/N	Examples of what I do to support minimalism	Barriers to my advocacy
Prioritize my students and their needs?			
Model the changes I want to see?			
Show how I under-stand the value that already exists?			
Share my stories?			

Figure 6.3
Minimalist Teacher Advocacy Action Plan

If I am not . . .	Then . . .	What I need to do now	How I can do this
Prioritizing my students and their needs			
Modeling the changes I want to see			
Showing how I understand the value that already exists			
Sharing my stories			

your purpose (e.g., providing quality education) and priorities (e.g., meeting student needs, engaging students in learning, etc.)?

With your organized thoughts, we can now move ahead to contemplate the areas in which you will be campaigning as you scoot along your path to the minimalist teacher life. By now we hope you are set to adopt a minimalist approach to teaching and know that advocating for it will provide a clearer path to more meaning in your teaching life.

Advocating for You: The Minimalist Teacher

When we advocate for our beliefs (providing meaningful education to students *and* decluttering our teaching space of erroneous programs and things), we plead a case for the relevancy of what is important in our lives. How can we do this?

Refocus on Relationships

We are writing this book in the midst of a health emergency, a pandemic—something we have never experienced in our lives. Why would we continue writing a book about decluttering teaching now? Because *now* is the penultimate moment in time for us, not only as teachers but as humans, to actually discover the purpose of education and be cognizant of our priorities within it. *Now* is the time to purposefully reevaluate what is most relevant in education. We've had many of the "unnecessities" that we talked about earlier stripped away, and what were we left with? We were left with our students. Just us and them.

So now think. When you made the shift from classroom teaching to teaching from home, did you grab a few pillowcases and scoop all of your classroom resources like a burglar in an attempt to seize precious jewels in a heist? Or did you think about tending to the basic needs of your own students? We are going to make an assumption that you zeroed in on ensuring that your students were OK, that their health and safety were your priority.

This is the time to advocate for less curriculum clutter and a greater focus on relationships. *This is the time* to think about what is useful and meaningful, and what has wasted our time and energy. *This is the time* when we can advocate for a cleaner, more streamlined way of teaching and learning by focusing on our students through a simpler yet more meaningful approach. Only then can you ask yourself, "What do I do now?"

Understanding Your Role and Your Context

An important element when considering how to lead change or advocate for a new approach is in the social backdrop of where you are working. Understanding the importance of social capital, how to make use of your interpersonal skills, and the people who surround you are going to be relevant factors in bringing about change. Who are you more likely to listen to about new changes in your approach to teaching: a friendly colleague who will listen and welcome you, or an aggressive colleague demanding acquiescence? Getting to know the professionals around you will make a difference in the way in which you will be able to get them on board.

Mihoko Chida has worked as a teacher, principal, team or cohort leader, and curriculum designer in California, Tokyo, and Bangkok. She highlights that she has felt like she has been able to advocate in all of the roles that she has held since her first years as a teacher. She says that the key elements are building relationships, naming and valuing positive skills in others, and modeling vulnerability. She has found that being intentional with how she navigates these soft influences is crucially important to positively influence your colleagues' growth. "I think that goes a long way in building relationships—just a genuine interest in the other person."

Think back to Chapter 3. We discussed how people are at different stages of adopting new ideas and initiatives. Get to know who those early adopters may be, and see if there is any interest in adopting a minimalist approach to education. Knowing your colleagues well, and identifying those who may fall into the laggard category, may be beneficial as well. You might gain valuable insight into their barriers to taking on these new ideas and assist those that may be having a harder time. They might just be the people who need it the most. Farina and Kotch (2008) stated, "Teachers change their beliefs and behavior when they are surrounded by supportive colleagues; when they see effective strategies in action; and when they are encouraged to take risks, reflect on their beliefs, and revise their approach to teaching every day" (p. 178).

Understand Your Global Impact and Responsibility

In *Less Stuff*, Lindsay Miles (2019) discusses how minimalism and reducing waste do not need to be mutually exclusive. In fact, decluttering and sustainable waste reduction can go hand in hand. When we have extraneous clutter in our lives, be it abstract or physical things, we are filled with waste. Whenever we are not using something to the utmost extent, that is a form of waste. However, when we use a framework such as Triple P, we can reevaluate all resources and reduce waste in all forms.

We can again visit teaching during a pandemic. As stated above, it is essential to meet the basic needs of students and refocus on relationships before asking ourselves what to do with students academically (even though the reaction was to get devices and just keep teaching!). Eventually, did you begin to think creatively about what you already had in your house to teach with, and what simple things students might have at home that they could use for learning? Did your focus shift from teacher-made toolkits to more home-based, student-created resources for their use—if it was needed? Perhaps you began to settle into the notion that you do not need papers or cutouts and began to rethink your use of physical resources, and the impact all of these unused resources have on our well-being and the world on a larger scale.

We are living in multiple global awareness movements, from climate action to social justice reform and totally transforming education. What we need to do now is focus on the mark we leave on our planet, and how we approach education with a mindset to reduce clutter can support this mindset. We hope that our strategies to zone in on teaching with meaning and transfer thinking across disciplines will help you center your thinking on the idea that we will have better prepared our students for a future in which they have truly received a quality education. This provides the potential for meaningful contributions to society through their innovative ideas and through creativity.

We can begin to recognize and understand our journey and role in creating so much waste when we peek into the United Nations Sustainable Development Goals (SDGs) (UN Department of Economic and Social Affairs, n.d.). These 17 goals require us to make drastic change on a global level, to come together to eradicate global and systemic inequalities and inequities. We can do that by advocating for quality education (SDG 4) or decluttering for responsible production and consumption (SDG 12). To learn more about how your shift to becoming a minimalist teacher aligns with the SDGs, you can visit https://sdgs.un.org/goals.

Simple Ways to Build in Advocacy Events for Minimalism at School

What are some simple ways to advocate for a minimalist approach in teaching and gather a group of like-minded individuals? Well, think about what it looks and sounds like when you advocate for something you believe in! You tell people. Don't overthink what advocacy looks and sounds like! Here are some suggestions.

1. **Raise awareness:** Share this approach to teaching and learning. Share what you learned in this book!

2. **Read the research:** There is plenty to read in terms of the benefits of minimalism and its effect on well-being. Share!

3. **Watch documentaries:** There is plenty to watch about the benefits of responsible consumption and its effect on our planet. We know we are in a global crisis, and there is plenty of research about how our plastics have made their way to the once-untouched Arctic.

4. **Have conversations:** Talk with your team about how you can make your teaching lives easier. Remember, like all important things, this does require commitment upfront. But working through the process is worth your increased mental clarity and decreased stress.

5. **Request a budget review:** Whether at the school or legislative level, budgets often go to things like new furniture or curriculum packages or technology rather than essential people and resources that can help develop and grow the school in meaningful ways.

In Conclusion

Chapter Takeaways

- There will be some challenges in moving forward with this approach, including feeling stuck, alone, scared, and overwhelmed.
- Completing an advocacy audit will help get ideas organized to ensure the proactive engagement in this cycle.

- Creating an action plan will support efforts to move forward and help you be accountable in sustaining this mindset.

Lingering Question

Who will I bring with me on this journey?

Up Next

In our concluding chapter, we wrap all parts of the Triple P framework back together and leave you with a few final thoughts about becoming a minimalist teacher.

Concluding Thoughts

Dichotomous thinking—believing that there is only one way or another, no in-between—is pervasive in education. Whole language versus phonics; STEM versus the arts; inclusion versus separatism. And this is nothing new. Back in 1938, John Dewey wrote in *Education and Experience* that "[m]ankind likes to think in extreme opposites" (p. 5). We want to throw this binary thinking out and be the first to exclaim that the Triple P framework is not the be-all and end-all on your path to minimalism in education. There may be elements of this approach we have discussed here that may not be prevalent in your culture, suit you right now, or fit the context in which you are currently working, but we invite you to read more widely and do some further reflection on your own. We hope that some of the authors and texts we have referenced throughout the book will now be on your go-to list.

You have worked through a series of Triple P funnels to help you find your purpose and organize your priorities so you can pare down your resources and effectively meet your desired priorities. We designed this funnel for aspects and roles of teaching life, yet it can be applied in your personal life as well (see Figure C.1).

Figure C.1
The Triple P Funnel

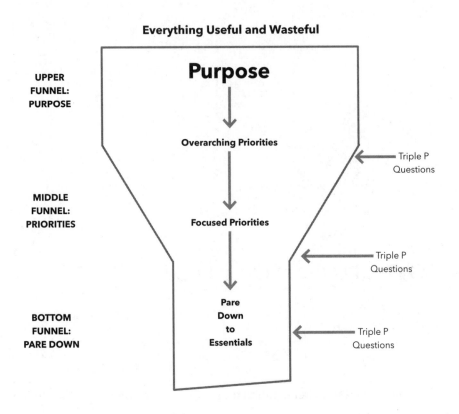

As you read through the chapters that suited your need, you would have seen our cycle icons marking various sections of texts (see Figure C.2). You would have seen the emphasis on beginning with ideas, inquiring, and investigating. It is essential that this takes place before acting. Acting without prior thought and consideration will undoubtedly result in further time, resource, and emotional waste. Rashly jumping in to act while decluttering will not result in lasting change toward a minimalist mindset. Informed and judicious action will allow for a durable response and will ensure the best foundation for advocating to your community.

As you move forward, we can consider those who may argue against a minimalist approach, as Gretchen Rubin (2019a) has in her book *Outer Order, Inner Calm*. In her view, the amount and type of physical possessions that people need within their spaces is going to be vastly different. So advocating to simply just have "less" is not very helpful. The key to minimalism is that

Figure C.2
The Triple P Cycle

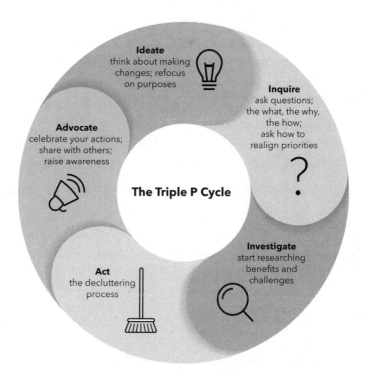

the items you do keep around you are ones you meaningfully engage with. We can extrapolate on this idea to all the elements of education that we have discussed here. Teaching will always be an overly busy job. But we encourage you to strive to ensure all those elements of "busyness" are ones in which there is meaning to you, that in fact do meet with your purpose and priorities. Let us take control in order to pare down what makes you busy without adding meaning or depth. Let's take a moment to review the Triple P framework that has guided us through this process toward minimalism in education:

- **Purpose:** When we prompt you to think about purpose, we really want you to reflect on the meaning behind the actions you are taking. When you identify your objective or goal, you will have better clarity as you begin to funnel into your priorities.

- **Priorities:** Your priorities are the items, tasks, and behaviors that should take precedence when working toward your purpose. These are your key concerns that should form the basis of your decisions and next steps. It is easy to see the crossovers in purpose, but as you sift through each part of your decluttering process, these become more focused as you prepare to pare down.

- **Pare Down:** Paring down is deliberately left as the final P in the Triple P framework. This is the action-oriented part of the cycle, and it also requires mental effort. It is only by considering your purpose and priorities that you can begin to cut back and curtail what is unnecessary and wasteful in your practice. There are a lot of ways we could misuse the precious time we have with our students and alongside our colleagues. Having your mind fixed on your true goals will aid in making the most of that time.

While we have outlined detailed processes to use the Triple P framework throughout this book, we hope that the simple idea of these three Ps will carry you through your work in your daily practice. Just like we use a mantra to remind ourselves of something important, so, too, can we use the Triple P framework each day. If you catch yourself in the clutter of your work, refer to the Triple P framework to remind yourself about how you really want to work. Feeling frustrated in a meeting? Feeling agitated with tasks left incomplete at the end of the day? Too many items on the to-do list? Give yourself a moment to step back and really consider your purpose, filter your priorities, and pare down what you are able to in order to refocus with a minimalist mindset.

Ultimately, minimalism is about our journey to finding "enough" as Miles (2019) has mentioned. We all have our own very personal version of enough: enough physical clutter, enough time consumption, enough new initiatives. While working your way through this book through the lens of the Triple P framework, we hope that you can find your own version of enough. We are confident that any educator can find the right balance between aspiring to be the best they can be as a teacher yet not overstep into feeling overwhelmed when committed to finding clarity.

In our final thoughts with you here, we would like to take a moment to discuss the importance of establishing and sustaining this practice. Going through the processes once will help, but returning to them regularly will be more powerful down the line. Just as we must practice repeatedly to develop skills, routines, and positive habits, so, too, do we need to work on a way toward minimalism as teachers. While the idea of "one-and-done" is appealing and inviting, this will not lead us to a sustainable shift in practice. We invite you to commit to doing this life-changing work as you shift from more to less. We ask that you vocalize your clarity and share your success to bring others into the journey of becoming a minimalist teacher. This shift can change the culture of teaching and learning and remind us of the true purpose of education.

Appendix A:
The Triple P Cycle

To support the greater vision of this process, we created the Triple P cycle (see Figure A.1). Thinking about the process as you work through it allows you to exercise your neurons in order to develop new habits in your teaching life. When we identify our place within a cycle, we become more reflective and engage in very deliberate decisions, a skill that corresponds to the "managing impulsivity" Habit of Mind (Costa, 2008). Being intentional is a key part of making a shift in approach. Our hope for you is to think more about your habits and how they help or hinder your effectiveness and efficiency.

Ideate: In the idea phase, you think about making changes in practice and want to refocus on the greater *purpose* of the work you do daily. This is a highly reflective and thought-provoking part of the cycle. You must have a clear purpose before lining up your priorities.

Inquire: In the inquire phase, you ask yourself and others questions about the *priorities* within different areas of teaching and learning. You ask about the what, why, and how of shifting practice and understand that priorities are essential to further investigation and eventually paring down.

Investigate: In the investigate phase, you start researching, reading, and understanding the benefits and challenges of working through the process of becoming a minimalist teacher. You investigate why others choose to go through this process and why this process is becoming a *priority* for you in your teaching life.

Action: The action phase is essentially *paring down*, or the decluttering process. This part of the process is all about decluttering all of your spaces—including your physical, mental, and emotional spaces—so you can reduce the stress and burden of too much of everything.

Advocate: The advocacy phase of the cycle is a celebration. This is a deliberate phase to celebrate your success and raise awareness of the benefits of this entire process. While advocating for minimalism in teaching may occur at any point during the cycle, you will likely work through the process yourself or with one colleague before you are truly ready to share your belief in this approach. But of course, we would be more than excited for you to bring as many colleagues into this process as you can!

Figure A.1
The Triple P Cycle

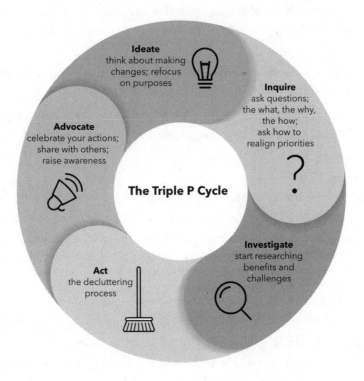

?

Appendix B: Initiatives, Purposes, and Priorities

Initiatives

All schools have educational initiatives. Because there are a range of initiatives from mandated to self-initiated, we wanted to provide you with a list of initiatives that may be in place or are in the process of getting implemented. Our goal with providing the list is for you to recognize the breadth of the initiative fatigue we experience and that when we weed through everything, you can find your way to the purpose or advocate for the removal of the clutter.

Mandated Initiatives: ultimately chosen by administrators due to district demands yet may have been evaluated by teachers. Although you may not be the decision maker in whether to adopt the program, there are decisions you can make within these initiatives. You can always question the purpose behind them within your context and identify your priorities. Once those elements are identified, you can weed through to choose your essential elements that match your purpose and priorities.

Examples:

- Specific social-emotional learning (SEL) programs
- Character education programs
- Science, technology, engineering, (arts), and math (STEM/STEAM) programs
- Behavioral management programs
- Specific teacher effectiveness rating systems
- After-school programming
- Technology integration
- Staff development such as "Leader in Me"
- Artists in residence
- Master Chef

School-based Initiatives: usually teacher-initiated but may be initiated by parents or students. As advocates of a less-is-more approach, we love the idea that teachers and students would be implementing initiatives in which they have been the decision makers, such as coming up with the idea of an initiative that has a positive influence on the student learning experience. When teachers and students have agency in this process, the purpose is tangible and aligned to priorities. Keeping the initiatives pared down may be a challenge in all the excitement! Stay focused!

Examples:

- Grading systems
- Parent involvement nights
- Science or math fair
- Bulletin board projects
- Student council or other student leadership groups
- Student-led clubs
- Literacy week activities
- Any kind of "-a-thon"
- Community organization involvement or charity work

Purposes

Sometimes the challenge lies in having a clear sense of purpose, which can be muddied like a puddle after a heavy rain with all we have flooding our teaching system. This list is not to overwhelm but instead to look at over-arching purposes in areas of your teaching life. This list may help you find a better-matched purpose when you work through your decluttering process. A focused purpose can help you zero in on your key priorities when working through your framework.

Purpose in teaching:
- To provide opportunities for learners to grow
- To provide access to knowledge
- To provide access to resources
- To provide awareness that we all have a responsibility as global citizens
- To provide opportunity for learners to have a voice in all aspects of their learning (from classroom setup to learning experiences)
- To provide anti-racist and anti-bias education
- To guide learning
- To facilitate interactions
- To facilitate relationships
- To support development of academic and life skills
- To support equitable access to opportunities
- To develop and equip a future generation of leaders

Purpose in learning:
- To be able to learn and use skills in a real-life context
- To learn how to interact with people appropriately
- To develop relationships with other learners
- To become aware of and understand one's responsibility as a global citizen
- To experience culturally relevant learning
- To develop personal knowledge and skills
- To realize potential

- To be exposed to different experiences and stories from beyond our own community

Purpose of environment:
- To provide a safe space for learning
- To provide a place in which learners feel a sense of belonging
- To stimulate thinking
- To have space for exploration and interaction with peers and resources
- To provide exposure in understanding that organized space is transferable to all life contexts

Purpose of initiatives:
- To add value to the existing culture or effectively used frameworks
- To create a shift in culture in order to move to more effective practices
- To create a consistency in the culture or environment
- To support a common vision, mission, and language
- To meet the mandates of the district or school
- To stay on target with educational trends
- To develop a better system for collecting student data school- or grade-wide
- To foster communication systems with parents and students
- To support your professional learning
- To develop student engagement practices
- To enhance the aesthetics of your school spaces

Purpose of curriculum:
- To provide a framework for teaching
- To provide benchmarking for grade levels
- To provide the "what" teachers teach
- To provide the "what" students should know, understand, and be able to do
- To provide culturally relevant content

Purpose of instruction:
- To engage all learners
- To teach dispositions, skills, and content in age-appropriate ways

- To allow for sparks of interest to develop and nurture them
- To provide culturally relevant learning experiences

Purpose of assessment:
- To gauge student understanding
- To inform further instruction
- To inform future planning
- To provide a framework for students to self-assess
- To provide a common language for strength and growth
- To provide bias-free opportunities for students to show learning
- To provide accountability in the teaching and learning cycle

Purpose of advocacy:
- To provide opportunities for having voices heard
- To raise awareness of a belief or cause
- To share ideas with others
- To enable discourse about what is important and relevant

Priorities

Like finding our clear purpose in all the work we do, coming up with pinpointed priorities can feel like listening to a record with a skip in it. Sometimes the challenge lies in having a clear sense of your priority with all we have flooding our teaching system. This list is not to overwhelm, but instead to tune into what your priorities really are. This list may help you find the right one (or two) or fine-tune your priorities when you work through your decluttering process. Just remember to link your top priority back to your purpose. Keep this focused and streamlined by only choosing one or two priorities when working through your framework.

Priorities in teaching:
- To build relationships with students
- To engage learners in age- and intellectually appropriate learning
- To be an anti-racist educator
- To be a learner
- To be a facilitator of learning

- To encourage positive interactions among students
- To attend to student needs
- To differentiate for learners
- To provide opportunities for learning based on student interest

Priorities in learning:

- To have fun
- To seek guidance to support learning
- To develop dispositions that support success like empathy
- To share learning with others
- To learn new content
- To practice and apply learned skills
- To attain new skills
- To learn from peers

Priorities of the physical environment:

- To provide a structured space for learners and learning
- To provide a space to house curated and appropriate materials for learning
- To provide a learning environment that supports accessibility and use of curated resources
- To provide equity in learning
- To have materials that represent learners as well as others that may not be in our immediate community
- To provide a space that invokes thinking, designing, and creation
- To allow students to engage in the organization and selection of resources for the space

Priorities in initiatives:

- To provide essential learning for staff
- To support effective practices that already exist
- To develop a better system for collecting student data, school- or grade-wide
- To foster communication systems with parents and students
- To support your professional learning

- To develop student engagement practices
- To update teaching practices

Priorities in curriculum:

- To ensure school communities know what to teach
- To scaffold or guide teachers to understand standards, content, or instructional practices
- To highlight the range in material resources
- To assist in planning to meet student needs and age-appropriate or development benchmarks
- To support the development of academic or social-emotional skills

Priorities in instruction:

- To provide age-appropriate teaching approaches for student learning
- To provide anti-racist and inclusive educational experiences
- To teach skills and content through an approach that develops dispositions for success
- To reach all learners in ways that meet their specific needs

Priorities in assessment:

- To learn student strengths
- To know areas that need support
- To remove barriers in assessment
- To provide bias-free opportunities for students to show learning
- To provide scaffolds for making improvements in misconceptions of learning
- To provide clarity in knowing and understanding areas of strength and needs for growth
- To provide opportunity for students to gain independence by identifying the supports they need

Priorities in advocacy:

- To raise awareness
- To uphold your beliefs
- To bring people together with a common goal
- To grow your support system

?

Appendix C:
The Minimalist Teacher
Book Study Guide

Are you stuck in a specific chapter or part of the Triple P cycle? Maybe it's a good time to call on your professional learning community for a book study. Reading together can clarify a vision and provide a common language for those wishing to engage in the great pursuit of deep, meaningful discussions. We will help you navigate and gain a sense that there are at least some tracks in the grass or a dirt road that you can follow. We can help you find your path to something that can result in a profound change in your teaching approach.

Introduction

1. Write one sentence that summarizes your initial thoughts when reading through the introduction.
2. How do you feel about shifting your current teaching approach to a minimalist approach?

3. What are the positives you anticipate for you and your students when making this shift?

4. What are you feeling nervous or apprehensive about?

5. Who is your accountability partner, and what is your plan for checking in with each other?

Chapter 1: Creating a Culture of Minimalism in Your Classroom

1. How would you describe your current classroom culture?

2. What do you envision your classroom to be while in the process of bringing a culture of minimalism to your students and into your teaching life?

3. What do you anticipate your greatest challenges will be in making a shift to minimalism in your classroom culture?

Chapter 2: Decluttering the Physical Environment

1. How do you feel about decluttering your physical environment? Why?

2. What is causing you the greatest anxiety or greatest feeling of joy as you take this on?

3. Gretchen Rubin argues against the idea that simply having less is not very helpful and that the key to minimalism is to keep the items that you meaningfully engage with. Share your thoughts about this idea and how it may help or hinder how you declutter your physical environment.

Chapter 3: Decluttering Initiatives

1. List all of your school's initiatives.

2. In what ways do you or can you influence school-based initiatives?

3. How do you envision a meaningful use of your school's initiatives?

4. How can you support your leadership team in (re)prioritizing initiatives?

5. How will you advocate for paring down initiatives?

6. Andrea, a middle school teacher with experience in Toronto, New York City, two schools in China, and Singapore, stated, "At the moment, I don't think that I've ever worked at a school that has supported minimalism, but I have worked at a lot of schools that value efficiency." Can you relate? How?

Chapter 4: Decluttering the Curriculum

1. What have you identified as your key purpose from your curricula?
2. In what ways does this align with your pedagogical beliefs?
3. How will you be filtering through and choosing your priorities?
4. What do you need to do for yourself with your team when decluttering your curriculum?

Chapter 5: Decluttering Instructional and Assessment Strategies

1. What is the key purpose behind your instruction and assessment?
2. What is it that you spend the most amount of time doing when planning and preparing learning experiences?
3. How do you ensure you use your time in the most effective ways?
4. What is your key priority during instructional time?
5. What is your key priority while students are learning with their peers or independently?
6. What do you think the hardest part of paring down your instruction will be?
7. What do you think the hardest part of paring down your assessment will be?
8. What is your priority for yourself and with your team?

Chapter 6: Advocating for Minimalism in Your Teaching Environment

1. Advocacy can be many different things. What will advocating for your new practice look like?

2. What are your top three takeaways that you tell someone about the process?

3. What is the most important reason you can think of that will push you to keep up with attaining your new habits as a minimalist teacher?

Historical and Cultural Ideas Around Minimalism

1. What are your thoughts about the origins of minimalism?

2. How do you envision creating a culture of minimalism yet still ensure you view your curriculum, instruction, and assessment with a trauma-sensitive and culturally informed lens?

References

Acree, Y. V. (2017, May 1). What are Black minimalists? *Black Minimalism.* Retrieved from https://blackminimalists.net/blog/what-are-black-minimalists

Agarwal, P. K., & Bain, P. M. (2019). *Powerful teaching: Unleash the science of learning.* San Francisco: Jossey-Bass.

Claxton, G. (2018). Learning friendly teacher action and talk. *Building Learning Power.* Retrieved from https://www.Buildinglearningpower. Com/2018/05/Learning-Friendly-Action-and-Talk/

Costa, A. (2008). Describing the Habits of Mind. In A. L. Costa & B. Kallick (Eds.), *Learning and leading with Habits of Mind: 16 essential character-istics for success* (pp. 15–41). Alexandria, VA: ASCD.

Couros, G., & Novak, K. (2019). *Innovate inside the box: Empowering learners through UDL and the innovator's mindset.* San Diego: IMPress Publishing.

de Bono, E. (2015). *Simplicity.* London: Penguin Books.

Dewey, J. (1938). *Education and experience.* New York: Macmillan.

Farina, C., & Kotch, L. (2008). *A school leader's guide to excellence: Collaborating our way to better schools.* Portsmouth, NH: Heinemann.

Gladwell, M. (2004, February 1). Choice, happiness and spaghetti sauce. [Video]. *TEDTalks*. Retrieved from https://www.ted.com/talks/malcolm_gladwell_choice_happiness_and_spaghetti_sauce?language=en

Glover, C. (2017, November 23). Is minimalism for Black people? *Pacific Standard*. Retrieved from https://psmag.com

Goldring, R., Taie, S., & Riddles, M. (2014, September). Teacher attrition and mobility: Results from the 2012-13 teacher follow-up survey. Retrieved from https://nces.ed.gov/pubs2014/2014077.pdf

Gonzalez, J. (2014, February 5). Meet the single point rubric. Retrieved from https://www.cultofpedagogy.com/single-point-rubric/

Gonzalez, J. (2018, March 18). 12 ways to upgrade your classroom design. Retrieved from https://www.cultofpedagogy.com/upgrade-classroom-design/

Hattie. J. (2009). Visible learning: Influences. Retrieved from http://www.visiblelearningmetax.com/Influences

Hendrick, C. (2017, October 27). Teachers: Your guide to learning strategies that really work. *The Guardian*. Retrieved from https://www.theguardian.com/teacher-network/2017/oct/27/teachers-your-guide-to-learning-strategies-that-really-work

Hyerle, D. N. (2011). *Student successes with thinking maps: School-based research, results, and models for achievement using visual tools* (2nd ed.). Thousand Oaks, CA: Corwin Press.

Johnson, B. (2019, November 17). Innovative leadership [Video]. Retrieved from https://www.youtube.com/watch?v=9JrXXEekrwY&t=287s

Knutsen, S. (2018, September 19). Work-life balance: Saying no can make you a better teacher. Retrieved from https://education.cu-portland.edu/blog/lifestyle/better-teacher-saying-no/

Lucchesi, E. L. B. (2019, January 11). The unbearable heaviness of clutter. Retrieved from https://www.nytimes.com/2019/01/03/well/mind/clutter-stress-procrastination-psychology.html?mc=adintl&ad-keywords=IntlAudDev&subid1=TAFI&dclid=CIT9zNmPmOECFZatyAodWF0BuQ

McKeown, G. (2014). *Essentialism: The disciplined pursuit of less*. London: Virgin Publishing.

McTighe, J., & Willis, J. (2019). *Upgrade your teaching: UbD meets neuroscience*. Alexandria, VA: ASCD.

Miles, L. (2019). *Less stuff: Simple zero-waste steps to a joyful and clutter-free life*. Melbourne: Hardie Grant Books.

Millburn, J. F., & Nicodemus, R. (2011). *Minimalism: Live a meaningful life*. Missoula, MT: Asymmetrical Press.

Muhammad, G. (2020). *Cultivating genius: An equity framework for culturally and historically responsive literacy*. New York: Scholastic.

Murdoch, K. (2020). Inquiry by the Fire [Video].

National Foundation for Educational Research. (2019). More teachers feel tense or worried about their job than those in comparable professions. Retrieved from https://www.nfer.ac.uk/news-events/press-releases/more-teachers-feel-tense-or-worried-about-their-job-than-those-in-com-parable-professions/

Neil, J. (2014). *Less > more: The ultimate guide to minimalist living: Declutter your life for happiness, health and organization.* Createspace Independent Publishing Platform.

Norton, A. (2018, November 18). Number of Americans practicing yoga, meditation surged in last six years. Retrieved from https://www.upi.com/Health_News/2018/11/08/Number-of-Americans-Practicing-Yoga-Meditation-Surged-in-Last-Six-Years/4871541738659/

O'Brien, B. (2019, April 5). Avoiding attachment: Buddhist teachings on letting go. *Learn Religions.* https://www.learnreligions.com/why-do-buddhists-avoid-attachment-449714

Ostroff, W. L. (2016). *Cultivating curiosity in K–12 classrooms: How to promote and sustain deep learning.* Alexandria, VA: ASCD.

Parr, K. (2014). Keep students and parents (and teachers) initiative fatigue free. Retrieved from http://www.wholechildeducation.org/blog/keep-students-and-parents-and-teachers-initiative-fatigue-free

Petricic, N. (2018, May 21). Teachers, we're operating with a scarcity mentality. *We Are Teachers.* Retrieved from https://www.weareteachers.com/abundance-mentality-for-teachers/

Platt, C. (2020, February 7). You can be a minimalist. Yes, you! TEDxCharlottesville. [Video]. Retrieved from https://www.youtube.com/watch?time_continue=140&v=tm8pvacsC_8&feature=emb_logo

Prochaska, J. O., & DiClemente, C. C. (2020, February 3). Transtheoretical model (or stages of change): Health behavior change. *Prochange.com.* Retrieved from https://www.prochange.com/transtheoretical-model-of-behavior-change

Rankin, J. G. (2016, November 22). The teacher burnout epidemic part 1 of 2. *Psychology Today.* Retrieved from https://www.psychologytoday.com/intl/blog/much-more-common-core/201611/the-teacher-burnout-epidemic-part-1-2

Ritchhart, R. (2015). *Creating cultures of thinking: The 8 forces we must master to truly transform our schools.* Hoboken, NJ: Wiley.

Robinson, K., & Aronica, L. (2015). *Creative schools: The grassroots revolution that's transforming education.* New York: Penguin Books.

Rogers, E. M. (2003). *Diffusion of innovations* (5th ed.). New York: Free Press.

Rubin, G. (2019a). *Outer order, inner calm: Declutter and organize to make more room for happiness.* New York: Harmony Books.

Rubin, G. (2019b, January 28). A yearly challenge: How to deal with post-holiday clutter? Here are my seven tips. Retrieved from https://gretchenrubin.com/2019/01/post-holiday-clutter-tips

Schwartz, B. (2005, July). *Barry Schwartz: The paradox of choice.* [Video file]. Retrieved from https://www.ted.com/talks/barry_schwartz_on_the_paradox_of_choice

Smith, D. (2017, October 21). Americans are getting outside in record numbers. *Wide Open Spaces.* Retrieved from https://www.wideopenspaces.com/americans-getting-outside-record-numbers/

Stephenson, J., Carter, M., & Wheldall, K. (2007). Still jumping on the balance beam: Continued use of perceptual motor programs in Australian schools. *Australian Journal of Education, 51*(1), 6–18.

Strauss, V. (2018, October 30). Why the reading wars are a waste of time. *Washington Post.* Retrieved from https://www.washingtonpost.com/education/2018/10/30/why-reading-wars-are-waste-time/?utm_term=.d07a322300b5

Sumeracki, M., Caviglioli, O., & Weinstein, Y. (2018). *Understanding how we learn: A visual guide.* New York: Routledge.

Thoonen, E. E., Sleegers, P. J., Oort, F. J., Peetsma, T. T., & Geijsel, F. P. (2011). How to improve teaching practices: The role of teacher motivation, organizational factors, and leadership practices. Retrieved from https://journals.sagepub.com/doi/abs/10.1177/0013161X11400185

UN Department of Economic and Social Affairs. (n.d.). United Nations Sustainable Development Goals. Retrieved from https://sdgs.un.org/goals

Watson, A. (2018, July 29). Classroom clutter—What to keep and what to toss. *The Cornerstone for Teachers.* Retrieved from https://thecornerstoneforteachers.com/truth-for-teachers-podcast/classroom-clutter-keep-toss/

Watson, A. (2019). *Fewer things, better: The courage to focus on what matters most.* New York: Due Season Press and Educational Services.

Wiliam, D. (2016, April). The secret of effective feedback. *Educational Leadership.* Retrieved from http://www.ascd.org/publications/educational-leadership/apr16/vol73/num07/The-Secret-of-Effective-Feedback.aspx

Index

The letter *f* following a page number denotes a figure.

About the Authors

Tamera Musiowsky-Borneman is an international education adviser, teacher coach, and classroom teacher who has taught and led in Singapore, New York City, and her home city of Edmonton, Canada. She is an ASCD Emerging Leader 2014 and past president of ASCD Emerging Leaders Alumni Affiliate (ELASCD). Tamera values simplicity and clarity in her life in general and thus has created a coaching model centered on the idea of coaching teachers in short, flexible, and focused chunks of time, with personalized content. Since 2015, Tamera has contributed content to a number of platforms such as ASCD Inservice, ASCD Express, Illinois ASCD's newsletter, EdWeek Teacher Blog, and Achieve the Core. She writes about student engagement, inclusion, agency, and ways to develop classroom and school culture. Her weekly blog posts are focused on organizing teaching spaces and can be found at tmused. com/blog. Connect with her on Twitter @TMus_Ed, or via e-mail at info@ tmused.com.

C. Y. Arnold is an Australian educator working both at home and abroad. She has worked in Australia, Japan, Singapore, and Belgium as a teacher, coach, mentor, co-teacher, coordinator, tutor, and supervisor from early childhood education to adult education in the university sector. Her dedication to the field of education has led her to serve on the board of the Singapore chapter of SENIA, publish educational articles, and present at various international and Australian conferences. Her interests in education include exploring research-based pedagogy and practice, inclusive education, quality early childhood education, inquiry, and promoting well-being for our students and teaching colleagues. You can follow her on Twitter @carnold005 or via e-mail at cyarnold.ed@gmail.com.

Tamera and C. Y. have coauthored other writing pieces for ASCD Inservice, ASCD Express, and *The Reformer* magazine. They have also presented workshops together at 21CL in Hong Kong and EARCOS/SENIA Teacher Conference in Bangkok, Thailand, about inclusive classroom practices that promote student agency.

Related ASCD Resources

At the time of publication, the following resources were available (ASCD stock numbers in parentheses).

Print Products

The Burnout Cure: Learning to Love Teaching Again by Chase Mielke (#119004)

Focus: Elevating the Essentials to Radically Improve Student Learning, 2nd Edition by Mike Schmoker (#118044)

Manage Your Time or Time Will Manage You: Strategies That Work from an Educator Who's Been There by PJ Caposey (#119005)

Mindfulness in the Classroom: Strategies for Promoting Concentration, Compassion, and Calm by Thomas Armstrong (#120018)

Never Work Harder Than Your Students and Other Principles of Great Teaching, 2nd Edition by Robyn R. Jackson (#118034)

Teach, Reflect, Learn: Building Your Capacity for Success in the Classroom by Pete Hall and Alisa Simeral (#115040)

The Teacher 50: Critical Questions for Inspiring Classroom Excellence by Baruti Kafele (#117009)

Teaching with Clarity: How to Prioritize and Do Less So Students Understand More by Tony Frontier (#121015)

For up-to-date information about ASCD resources, go to **www.ascd.org**. You can search the complete archives of Educational Leadership at **www.ascd.org/el**.

ASCD myTeachSource®

Download resources from a professional learning platform with hundreds of research-based best practices and tools for your classroom at http://myteachsource.ascd.org

For more information, send an e-mail to member@ascd.org; call 1-800-933-2723 or 703-578-9600; send a fax to 703-575-5400; or write to Information Services, ASCD, 1703 N. Beauregard St., Alexandria, VA 22311-1714 USA.

THE WHOLE CHILD

The ASCD Whole Child approach is an effort to transition from a focus on narrowly defined academic achievement to one that promotes the long-term development and success of all children. Through this approach, ASCD supports educators, families, community members, and policymakers as they move from a vision about educating the whole child to sustainable, collaborative actions.

The Minimalist Teacher relates to the **engaged**, **supported**, and **challenged** tenets.

For more about the ASCD Whole Child approach, visit **www .ascd.org/wholechild.**

WHOLE CHILD
TENETS

1 HEALTHY
Each student enters school healthy and learns about and practices a healthy lifestyle.

2 SAFE
Each student learns in an environment that is physically and emotionally safe for students and adults.

3 ENGAGED
Each student is actively engaged in learning and is connected to the school and broader community.

4 SUPPORTED
Each student has access to personalized learning and is supported by qualified, caring adults.

5 CHALLENGED
Each student is challenged academically and prepared for success in college or further study and for employment and participation in a global environment.

Become an ASCD member today!
Go to www.ascd.org/joinascd
or call toll-free: 800-933-ASCD (2723)

DON'T MISS A SINGLE ISSUE OF ASCD'S AWARD-WINNING MAGAZINE,

EL EDUCATIONAL LEADERSHIP

If you belong to a Professional Learning Community, you may be looking for a way to get your fellow educators' minds around a complex topic. Why not delve into a relevant theme issue of *Educational Leadership*, the journal written by educators for educators.

Subscribe now, or buy back issues of ASCD's flagship publication at **www.ascd.org/ELbackissues.**

Single issues cost $7 (for issues dated September 2006–May 2013) or $8.95 (for issues dated September 2013 and later). Buy 10 or more of the same issue, and you'll save 10 percent. Buy 50 or more of the same issue, and you'll save 15 percent. For discounts on purchases of 200 or more copies, contact **programteam@ascd.org**; 1-800-933-2723, ext. 5773.

To see more details about these and other popular issues of *Educational Leadership*, visit **www.ascd.org/ELarchive.**

1703 North Beauregard Street
Alexandria, VA 22311-1714 USA

www.ascd.org/el